NEW MEXICO
Territorial Era Caricatures

NEW MEXICO
Territorial Era Caricatures

Ron Hamm

SUNSTONE PRESS
SANTA FE

Images in this book from *New Mexico Men of Affairs in Caricature: The Optic Cartoon Book*, appear courtesy of the Center for Southwest Research and Special Collections, University Libraries, University of New Mexico.

© 2014 by Ron Hamm
All Rights Reserved.

No part of this book may be reproduced in any form or by any electronic or mechanical means including information storage and retrieval systems without permission in writing from the publisher, except by a reviewer who may quote brief passages in a review.

Sunstone books may be purchased for educational, business, or sales promotional use. For information please write: Special Markets Department, Sunstone Press, P.O. Box 2321, Santa Fe, New Mexico 87504-2321.

Book and Cover design › Vicki Ahl
Body typeface › ITC Benguiat Std
Printed on acid-free paper
∞
eBook 978-1-61139-229-6

Library of Congress Cataloging-in-Publication Data

Hamm, Ron, 1935-
  New Mexico territorial era caricatures / by Ron Hamm.
       pages cm
  Caricatures from H.S. Palmer's New Mexico men of affairs in caricature : the Optic cartoon book, published by Las Vegas Optic, in 1906.
  Includes bibliographical references and index.
  ISBN 978-0-86534-980-3 (softcover : alk. paper)
  1. New Mexico--Biography. 2. Caricatures and cartoons--New Mexico. 3. Politicians--New Mexico--Caricatures and cartoons. 4. Businessmen--New Mexico--Caricatures and cartoons. I. Palmer, H. S. (Harry S.), -1955. II. Palmer, H. S. (Harry S.), -1955. New Mexico men of affairs in caricature. III. Title.
  F795.H364 2014
  978.9--dc23
                                                    2013043965

WWW.SUNSTONEPRESS.COM
SUNSTONE PRESS / POST OFFICE BOX 2321 / SANTA FE, NM 87504-2321 /USA
(505) 988-4418 / ORDERS ONLY (800) 243-5644 / FAX (505) 988-1025

To Holm O. Bursum, a most Prominent Man of Affairs, and to his grandson Holm O. Bursum III and great grandson Holm O. Bursum IV for helping make this book possible.

CONTENTS

Acknowledgements 9
Introduction 11

William H. Andrews	24	Owen N. Marron	105
A.B. Baca	26	William E. Martin	108
Elfego Baca	29	James G. McNary	112
Charles L. Ballard	34	William J. Mills	115
Howard H. Betts	38	E.G. Murphey	118
Christopher N. Blackwell	41	William H. Newcomb	120
F.O. Blood	44	Miguel A. Otero	123
Walter S. Bowen	46	Frank W. Parker	127
Henry D. Bowman	48	Frederick H. Pierce	131
Cony T. Brown	50	William C. Porterfield	133
William A. Buddecke	54	George W. Prichard	136
William B. Bunker	56	Robert C. Rankin	138
Holm O. Bursum	58	James W. Raynolds	141
Edward A. Cahoon	63	Joshua S. Raynolds	145
Max Frost	66	A.B. Renehan	148
William H. Greer	72	Cleofes Romero	153
John E. Griffith	75	Eugenio Romero	156
Hiram Hadley	79	Secundino Romero	159
Herbert J. Hagerman	83	Hugo Seaberg	163
Willard S. Hopewell	86	Arthur Seligman	169
R.W. Hopkins	89	Willard S. Strickler	172
William P. Johnson	92	Robert M. Turner	174
W.A. Fleming Jones	94	John Howard Vaughn	176
W.H.H. Llewellyn	96	William B. Walton	178
Solomon Luna	100	George W. Ward	181

Suggested Further Reading 183

Acknowledgements

It has been said that it takes a village to raise a child. To a lesser degree it takes a sizeable community of experts and enthusiasts to help make a book, certainly one such as this. To that end, I wish to sincerely recognize every last one of the truly gifted and dedicated individuals who have helped me write this book. They are listed in alphabetical order, not in order of the importance of their contributions. The exception is my four-footed friend Smokie, who provided mostly silent companionship and offered a choice comment or two regarding usage and punctuation, often at five in the morning when his boss and mine, Peggy, was still abed until a more civilized hour. Then she jumped in. So it her book too.

So it is to a host of incredibly responsive, knowledgeable archivists, librarians, and other professionals around the state who pitched in with alacrity and aplomb to my sometimes frantic requests for help. They include Susan Berry, former Director of the Silver City Museum; Irisha A. Corral, Library Associate at the Thomas G. Donnelly Library at New Mexico Highlands University; Larry Creider, Director of Archives and Special Collections at New Mexico State University; Rob Dean, Editor of the *Santa Fe New Mexican*; Bob Eveleth, Senior Mining Engineer Emeritus with the New Mexico Bureau of Geology and Mineral Resources; Elvis E. Fleming of the Chaves County Historical Society; Linda Gegick, Museum Administrator, City of Las Vegas Museum; Chris Geherin, digger extraordinaire at the Center for Southwest Research and Special Collections at the University of New Mexico; Kelsey Grubb, Special Collections, Albuquerque-Bernalillo

County–Library; Royce Grubic for superb proofing and editing; Wayne Gunn for help with the Introduction ; Mary Holloway of the Inter-Library Loan Department at the Miller Library at Western New Mexico University, another searcher of great talent; John LeMay with the Chaves County Historical Society; Jesus L. Lopez, attorney and historian of Las Vegas; Michael Lord; A.B. Renehan descendant who supplied intriguing background on his ancestor; Bruce Wilson for the outstanding bibliography; Chellee Saiz, computer and software whiz; David Schneider, Southwest History Researcher with the Albuquerque-Bernalillo Library; and Silver City Museum volunteer research assistants. And to Faith Yoman of the New Mexico State Library, who was the first to help me. Then there was the Socorro funeral home director who walked through his city cemetery to try to locate the headstone of one of the subjects or the Las Vegas funeral home director who pored through old burial records, and the Masonic official who scoured his lodge's records to find information of a long dead former lodge brother. Gold star recipients for service above and beyond the call are Bob, Bruce, Chellee, Chris, Mary, and Wayne. You all know how much you helped. And finally to Jim Smith of Sunstone Press who had faith in this project and who helped me bring the *Optic Cartoon Book* to life again after more than a century in obscurity. To all of these wonderfully kind and helpful people, I say thank you.

Introduction

I suppose all writing projects are personal. This one certainly is. It was while writing another book, *The Bursums of New Mexico: Four Generations of Leadership and Service*, that Holm O. Bursum III showed me a dog-eared photocopy of an oddly sized book called *New Mexico Men of Affairs in Caricature: The Optic Cartoon Book* by H. S. Palmer. As soon as I began leafing through it, I was intrigued by the simplicity but the power of the drawings. They were clean, they were modern, they were warm. They depicted men who were someone's husband, father, or brother. I recognized some of the truly important names from New Mexico history (Holm O. Bursum was one, hence his grandson sharing his photocopy with me); other names I did not. I promised myself that when the Bursum project was finished, I would seek to rescue these caricatures from the oblivion into which they had fallen. I wanted to share them with other people. Fortunately, Holm Bursum III and his son Holm Bursum IV shared my enthusiasm and volunteered to help back the project. When it came to looking for a publisher, Sunstone Press was the obvious candidate. Its president, James Clois Smith, Jr., agreed.

The original book

I have been able to find only two copies of the actual book. They are both held by the Center for Southwest Research and Special Collections at the University of New Mexico. (The World Catalog lists a third copy as part of the holdings of the Thomas Branigan Memorial Library in Las Cruces, but the reference librarian there reports that it cannot be found.) I vividly recall the excitement I felt when the Center's Chris Geherin brought out its copies for me to examine. It was also the beginning of another warm and productive association; Chris could not have been more helpful.

The Center has graciously permitted us to reproduce the drawings, but what you are holding is not a facsimile of the book itself. That would have produced too unwieldy a work for the modern market. The original consists of twenty-six unbound sheets measuring 12.5" high by 16.5" wide (32 x 47 cm.): a striking four-color watercolor title page (possibly hand colored) and twenty-five heavy, cream-colored sheets holding two caricatures per sheet, mounted side by side on one side only. In one of the copies the drawings have a black matte; in the other they have a chocolate brown backing. Two holes were punched into the left side of each page, and the whole was held together by a decorative cord.

There is no indication within the book of how many copies were printed, nor any indication of how they were distributed. Did copies go only to the subscribers (of which more in a moment), or were they made available to the public as well? One oddity, due to the books being tied with cord, is that the order of the caricatures is not the same in the two copies. The photocopy has yet another sequence. The present edition reproduces the drawings in alphabetical order by the subject's name, and with only one caricature per page.

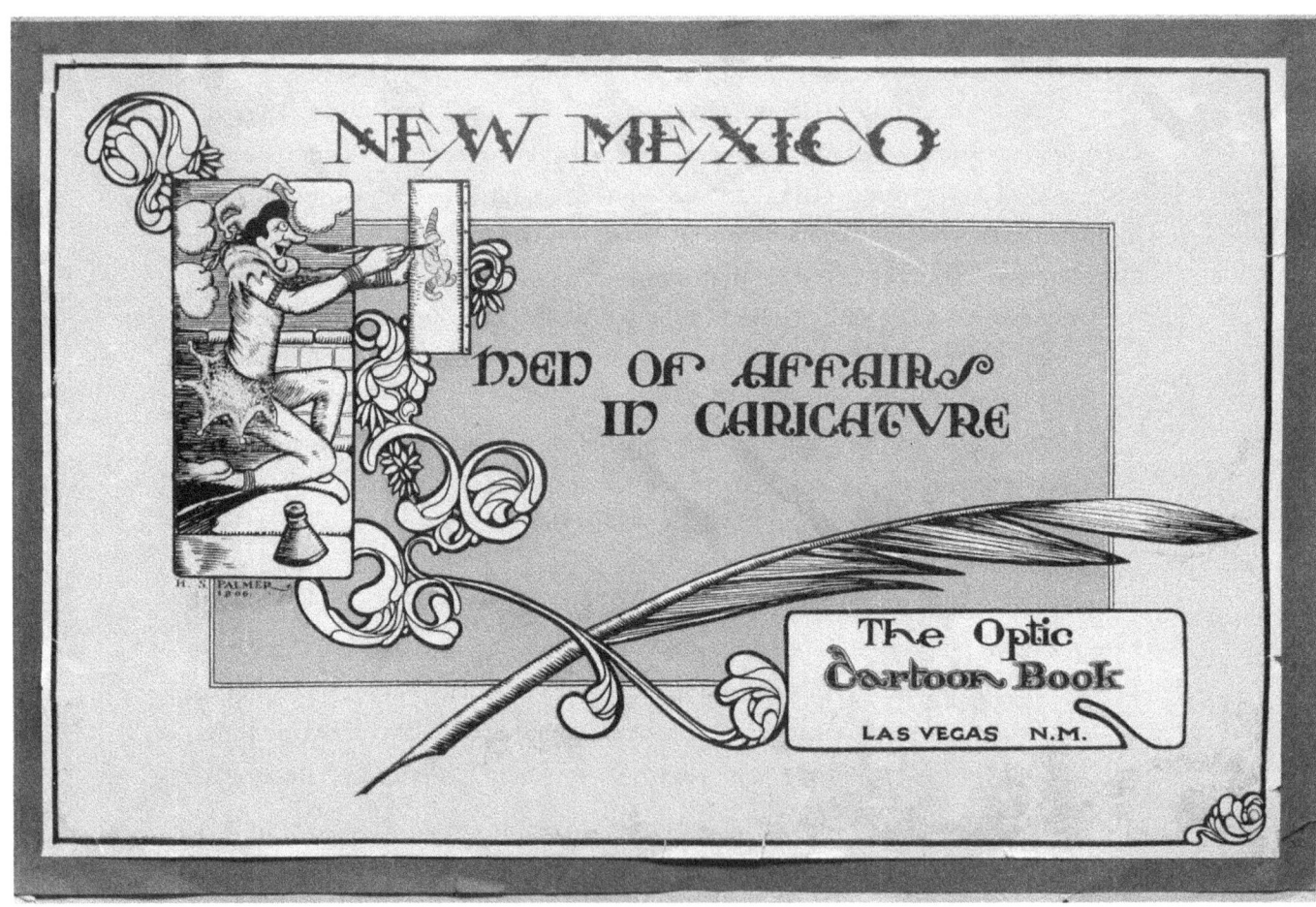

Original Cover

The book's origins

Where did the original book come from? The title page lists Las Vegas, New Mexico, and the year 1906. The subtitle offers another clue. As a former journalist myself, I knew that the major Las Vegas newspaper is still *The Optic*. So it made sense to look to its files for more information. I secured the microfilm for the newspaper for that year from the New Mexico State Library and worked my way through it with the generous aid of Mary Holloway of the Western New Mexico University Inter-Library Loan Department. Even though Las Vegas had a population of only five to six thousand in 1906, it was an important, growing city as the regional headquarters of the Santa Fe Railroad. In addition, the railroad's famed Montezuma Hotel was just a short distance away in Hot Springs.

The *Optic*—official name *Las Vegas Daily Optic*—was an afternoon newspaper, although it printed special morning editions for truly momentous events. It was bursting with news from around the territory, especially the burning issue of its move towards statehood, and from around the world (the latter brought in over the wires of the Associated Press), as well as pages of local news and abundant advertising. It could and did compete with its big city cousins, the *Santa Fe New Mexican* and the *Albuquerque Morning Journal*. The *Optic* was a much better newspaper than many of its contemporary, larger counterparts.

Sure enough: on February 12, 1906, there appeared a front-page notice announcing that the newspaper would launch a series of "cartoons of prominent and progressive men who are identified with the commercial development of this section." The first caricature appeared on February 17 of Kentucky transplant Frederick H. Pierce. It was followed by others at irregular intervals through April 12. For twelve days coverage of the San Francisco earthquake bumped the series out of newspaper altogether so readers could follow the events in that stricken city. The caricatures resumed on April 24 and ran through June 2. An unexplained gap then occurs until July 21. There are no more until August 4, the only one that month. The last two appeared on September 19 and September 28. The last was of Territorial Congressional Delegate William H. Andrews.

There was a total of thirty-three, generally two a week, sometimes more often and sometimes less. They were always on the front page. They appeared every day of the week except Sunday, when the newspaper did not publish. There was no accompanying headline on the profile, only a caption under the caricature. Unlike the resulting book, all but the last drawing were accompanied by a profile of the subject's life. [1]

These were written by the *Optic* owner and editor, James Graham McNary. In his autobiography, *This is My Life*, McNary writes that he had found "it uphill work" making ends meet and earning a living for his family. He thus "devised a scheme to bring in a few extra thousands of dollars. An artist by the name of H. S. Palmer sold me on the idea of printing an album of prominent New Mexico men of affairs." To this end he sought out subscribers who would be willing to pay $100 in order to have a drawing of their likeness published. That was actually a great deal of money at a time when that sum would buy an entire building lot in a small New Mexican town or several good men's suits, advertised in the *Optic* at just $12.50 apiece. McNary records, "I contacted about three score of the New Mexico leaders in politics, banking, and other lines of business, and we were finally successful in signing up about fifty...." McNary almost certainly used his well-connected father-in-law, Joshua S. Raynolds, president of The First National Bank of Albuquerque, Las Vegas, and El Paso, as he sought maximum participation.

The book's subjects

How did McNary choose his subscribers? Given that no public notice seems to have appeared in the *Optic*, it is logical to presume that it was by personal invitation only. Some of the subjects, already well-known in 1906, later became even better known. Holm O. Bursum, for example, went on to become a United States Senator. Justice William J. Mills became Governor. Perhaps Bursum was already anticipating his first run for Governor (in 1911) when he decided to have his likeness appear. He was the first non-Las Vegan to appear in the newspaper series. The subjects, in fact, came from just a handful of cities and towns. Inclusion was about equally divided among Las Vegas, Santa Fe, and Albuquerque, with about ten each. It was logical that Las Vegas would be so well represented since it was the place where McNary had his power base and where he published his book.[2] Socorro had six, Silver City five, Las Cruces three, and Raton and Roswell two each.

They represented chiefly two professions: law and commerce, along with a smattering of other endeavors, but there were no doctors or clergymen. They were mostly Republicans. Given McNary's political persuasion, that is not entirely unexpected. Seven subjects bore Spanish surnames, the rest Anglo. There were no Native Americans, no African Americans, and no women. It just would not have occurred to anyone to include them. There were native born and immigrants from other states, but only three foreign born and only two Anglos born in New Mexico. Several used honorifics such as "Colonel" because they had been given that rank when they were named to a governor's staff, but only six had earned legitimate active military rank. Still, some were former Rough Riders, naturally enough since New Mexico had sent five troops off to the Spanish American War.

The book's subjects share a common attribute: they were movers and shakers, if not in the territory, then in their home towns. Catholic, Jew; Yankee,

Rebel; Republican, Democrat; Anglo, Hispanic; native born and foreigner—all helped shape New Mexico in some way or other. The territory was a small place in 1906, so it is not surprising that their lives intertwined and came together in various ways. When the next census was taken in New Mexico in 1910, four years after the book appeared, it had a population of only 327,301; so chances were good that if you were Anglo, Republican, and a Mason you would encounter others like you somewhere, sometime.

One striking omission from the book is Thomas B. Catron. One of the richest, most powerful and influential men in the territory, Catron certainly could have afforded the $100. Perhaps Catron did not think it was worth it. Or maybe it was because he and Bursum were political rivals. Albert B. Fall is another prominent politician who is missing. Three of the men whose caricatures and profiles were included in the *Optic*—O.A. Larrazolo (later to be Governor and United States Senator), Ralph Emerson Twitchell, and Robert J. Taupert—were not included in the book. Perhaps they had changed their minds, or perhaps they did not pay the $100 fee for inclusion.

To recapitulate: Thirty-three drawings by Palmer appeared in the newspaper, all but one accompanied by a brief biography written by McNary. Thirty of these, plus twenty more seen for the first time (including one of McNary himself), were reproduced in the book. A profile of the editor accompanies his caricature within the present book.

Note: The spellings accompanying the caricatures are not always correct. They are correct in the author's text, however.

The artist

Harry Samuel Palmer is much more elusive than James Graham McNary. That front page notice in the *Optic* on February 12, 1906, is the first public record of any kind that I can find concerning him. It identifies the person responsible for the drawings as "Mr. H. S. Palmer, the celebrated cartoonist and newspaper illustrator, late of the *New York Journal* and *Pittsburg Press*." A search turns up no record of Palmer's work at the *Journal* or the *Press*, not surprising since he must have been in his early twenties at the time. Curiously, there is nothing to prove that he ever resided in Las Vegas either. Perhaps he stayed briefly at a hotel or in a boarding house, but his name is missing from the city directory printed by McNary as another source of income. (Two other Palmers do—one a tailor and one a painter.)

It is not clear how Palmer arrived at making his drawings. Did he work from photographs? Or did he actually visit each subject and sketch him live? That is unlikely because of the expense involved with travel. His style is generally straightforward, but it is sometimes whimsical, the subjects occasionally depicted in garb that they might typically wear on the job rather than in a formal situation. The men apparently had no objections to how they were depicted, or in the case of the newspaper profiles, to what was written about them. It would not have been in McNary's or Palmer's best interests, of course, to depict them in anything less than an acceptable, if not indeed flattering, light. By the way, the little gargoyle-type creature with doglike features inked in bottom corners of the drawings, was a feature common to newspaper cartoons of the time.

After the cartoonist finished his work for the *Optic*, he next surfaces in Boise, Idaho, in 1907. He was lured there by prospects of a short-term but steady paycheck and by expectations of national exposure to provide sketches for various newspapers covering the sensational trial of William D. (Big Bill) Haywood and others, including Harry Orchard. They had been charged in the bloody assassination on December 30, 1905, of former Idaho Governor, Frank Steunenberg. Returning home from a walk in the early evening hours, the governor opened the gate to his home in Caldwell, Idaho, and was blown into the air by a bomb. Bleeding profusely, he was carried into his home and died an hour later. Steunenberg was targeted because he had been governor in the aftermath of violent protracted labor violence at the silver mines in Coeur d'Alene in 1896. His call to President William McKinley for federal troops to quell the violence outraged the miners. Dynamite, a stock in trade of their profession, took on a more sinister role in their union struggles. The trial provided front page headlines in newspapers from coast to coast. Famed attorney Clarence Darrow came from Chicago to represent Orchard (who was sentenced to hang, then commuted to life imprisonment). "The Idanha Witness to History" website contains a drawing of Orchard from the *Evening Capitol News* attributed to Palmer. The site also contains another in his style, but it is not identified as by him.

Then once again Palmer seems to drop out of sight. Bruce Wilson, a history teacher at Western New Mexico University who generously offered to help me in my pursuit of the artist, discovered that he was on the East Coast by 1915. There he becomes one of the pioneers in American film animation. Most of his work involved shorts, two minutes or so in length. According to the Internet Movie Database, he directed seventy-eight films, wrote seventy-nine scripts, and produced another seventy-four films in an incredibly productive short span of time. Wilson found that one of Palmer's films, "The Siege of Liege" (1915), was the first in a series produced by MINA Cartoons. In 1915 or 1916 Palmer wrote a comedy for Budd Ross, an actor in some of the early Laurel and Hardy films. Palmer also appears as subject or as writer for at least eight articles in *Motion Picture World* and the *New York Dramatic Mirror* magazines between 1914 and 1916.

History of Animation, a two-disk DVD set containing twenty-one cartoons made between 1900 and 1921, has two humorous clips in which Palmer did both the animation and direction. They are "Women's Styles" (2 minutes, 51 seconds) and "Men's Styles" (3 minutes, 37 seconds). Two of his shorts can also be found on the Internet: "Keeping Up with the Joneses" and "I'm Insured." Both are introduced with a view of an artist's hands (presumably Palmer's) drawing them. One of the ironies of my search is that, for someone who devoted much of his professional career to executing likenesses of others, I have been unable to unearth any likeness of him, drawing or photograph. Unless of course Palmer caricaturized himself on the cover.

Palmer showed his litigious side when he was involved in a lawsuit with prominent fellow animator John Randolph Bray in 1916 concerning alleged patent infringement. Palmer had been working on the *Keeping Up with the Joneses* series when he lost a patent infringement suit to Bray over the use of transparent celluloid sheets. That series earned Palmer a mention in "Notable Cartoons" in *History of Animation* for his "Dancing Lessons" which was the first of the *Keeping Up with the Jones* series 1915-1916. He was also mentioned in "Notable Cartoons" for "Our National Vaudeville" in the first *Kartoon Komics* series in 1916–1917.

Donald Crafton, Professor of Film and Culture at the University of Notre Dame and author of the seminal work on early American film animation, *Before Mickey: The Animated Film 1898–1928*, cites Palmer's work several times, including a reproduction of a still from his best known "Professor Bonehead Is Shipwrecked." Denis Gifford mentions Palmer four times in his book, *American Animated Films; The Silent Era, 1897–1929*.

Then Palmer's public record again goes as blank as a movie screen when the feature ends. I can find nothing about him before he turns up for his final bow in Felice Levy's *Obituaries on File*. (Facts on File, 1979) There we learn that Harry Samuel Palmer died on August 17, 1955, in Miami, Florida, at the age of seventy-two. His profession is listed as "cartoonist." He does not appear in the Social Security Death Index.[3]

The present book

What Palmer and McNary conceived more than one hundred years ago in the small New Mexico Territory town of Las Vegas to make money for the two of them and to provide exposure for its subjects now takes on a second life, courtesy of an innovative and adventurous press located in the capital of the state that has just celebrated its centennial. Here are all fifty of the drawings in the original book. Many of the fifty are familiar faces, their position in New Mexico history secure. But sadly, for a few of the fifty, all that seems to remain are the likenesses and their names. Rather than reproduce the incomplete and necessarily unfinished biographies published in the newspaper, Jim Smith asked me to develop them all anew. To some extent, the length of my profile depends upon the material available.

Prominent or obscure, celebrated or forgotten, these figures collectively provide a richer picture of one aspect of New Mexico just six years shy of becoming a state in a way that formal, staged photographs cannot possibly offer. They should delight the art connoisseur and the history buff in equal measure. I am happy to offer Holm O. Bursum III, not exactly a replacement, but rather a complement to that well used photocopy he so serendipitously brought out to show me a couple of years ago.

Notes

1. The caricatures and their accompanying profiles appeared as follows: Saturday, February 17 (Frederick H. Pierce); Tuesday, February 20 (William A. Buddecke); Thursday, February 22 (George W. Ward); Saturday, February 24 (Cleofes Romero); Wednesday, February 28 (Ralph Emerson Twitchell, does not appear in the book); Saturday, March 3 (H. O. Bursum); Tuesday, March 6 (Herbert J. Hagerman); Thursday, March 8 (William B. Bunker); Tuesday, March 13 (Hiram Hadley); Thursday, March 15 (Willard S. Hopewell); Saturday, March 17 (Miguel A. Otero); Tuesday, March 20 (Christopher N. Blackwell); Thursday, March 22 (Eugenio Romero); Saturday, March 24 (Robert J. Taupert, does not appear in the book); Tuesday, March 27 (James W. Raynolds); Thursday, March 29 (Secundino Romero); Thursday, April 5 (William H. Greer); Saturday, April 7 (F. O. Blood); Thursday, April 12 (Edward A. Cahoon); Tuesday, April 24 (Robert C. Rankin); Saturday, May 5 (Joshua S. Raynolds); Wednesday, May 16 (Howard H. Betts); Saturday, May 19 (Walter S. Bowen); Tuesday, May 22 (Hugo Seaberg); Friday, May 25 (William E. Martin); Saturday, May 26 (Charles A. Ballard); Wednesday, May 30 (Arthur Seligman); Thursday, May 31 (George W. Prichard); Saturday, June 2 (William H. Newcomb); Saturday, July 21 (Willard S. Strickler); Saturday, August 4 (Max Frost); Wednesday, September 19 (A. O. Larrazolo, does not appear in the book); Friday, September 28 (William H. Andrews, without a profile). It is possible that the last is missing a profile because the New Mexico Republican Convention, in which Andrews played a key role, opened the next day in Las Vegas.

2. One point of clarification: there were two Las Vegas municipal entities in 1906. The original Las Vegas, west of the Gallinas River, was inhabited by those of Hispanic descent. When the railroad came in 1879 residents of the village that sprang up a mile east of the river were living in East Las Vegas and were Anglo. (An early editor of the *Optic* proudly proclaimed that his town was "American.") I refer to both cities as just Las Vegas.

3. As an illustration of the pitfalls of this kind of research, once earlier I was sure I had found what happened to Palmer after his animation stint. In searching the records Bruce Wilson discovered that a man named Harry Palmer drowned near Sydney, Australia, in 1920. His companion was the noted Australian cartoonist Claude Marquet. Was not it possible that the American had been Down Under visiting a friend in the same profession? Could they not have been out for an afternoon on the water? It all seemed to fit together—until Mary Holloway discovered that the drowned Harry Palmer was a local grocer. The pair had been returning by small craft with a load of supplies for his shop when tragedy struck.

DELEGATE TO CONGRESS. WM. H. ANDREWS,
ALBUQUERQUE

William H. Andrews: Territorial Delegate to Congress

William H. "Bull" Andrews had been a member of both chambers of the legislature in his home state of Pennsylvania when he was turned out of office. He cast his eyes west and came to New Mexico to seek further political success.

Andrews had held high office in his native Keystone State, according to "The Political Graveyard." He served first as Secretary of the Pennsylvania Republican Party for two years, then in the Pennsylvania State House of Representatives for three terms, and then in the Pennsylvania State Senate from 1895 until 1898.

Four years later, Andrews moved to Sierra County, New Mexico, and then to Albuquerque. There he established a power base and took up in Republican politics in New Mexico where he had left off in Pennsylvania but with even more spectacular results. He quickly became "an astute and dominant politician in New Mexico," according to the Center for Southwest Research at the University of New Mexico.

Andrews was a political ally of Holm O. Bursum, New Mexico Republican Party powerhouse, who managed his successful Congressional campaigns. Andrews served four terms in the 59th, 60th, 61st, and 62nd Congresses as the Delegate from New Mexico from March 4, 1905, until March 3, 1913. He was influential in the successful push for statehood.

Not everyone was an admirer. Elfego Baca of 'Frisco Shootout' fame certainly was not. A chapter entitled "Bull' Andrews Descends on New Mexico" in *Law and Order Ltd*. by Kyle S. Crichton is a clue. If the chapter is not clear enough, Baca clarifies his feelings by charging that Andrews "corrupted New Mexico," alleging that he was involved in vote-buying schemes as he and others sought various elective offices.

The Center for Southwest Research writes that Andrews organized the Pennsylvania Development Company, which built the New Mexico Central Railroad. He was later blamed for a $300,000 shortage in a Pennsylvania bank, money allegedly used to finance the railroad.

Andrews returned to his home state where he died January 16, 1919.

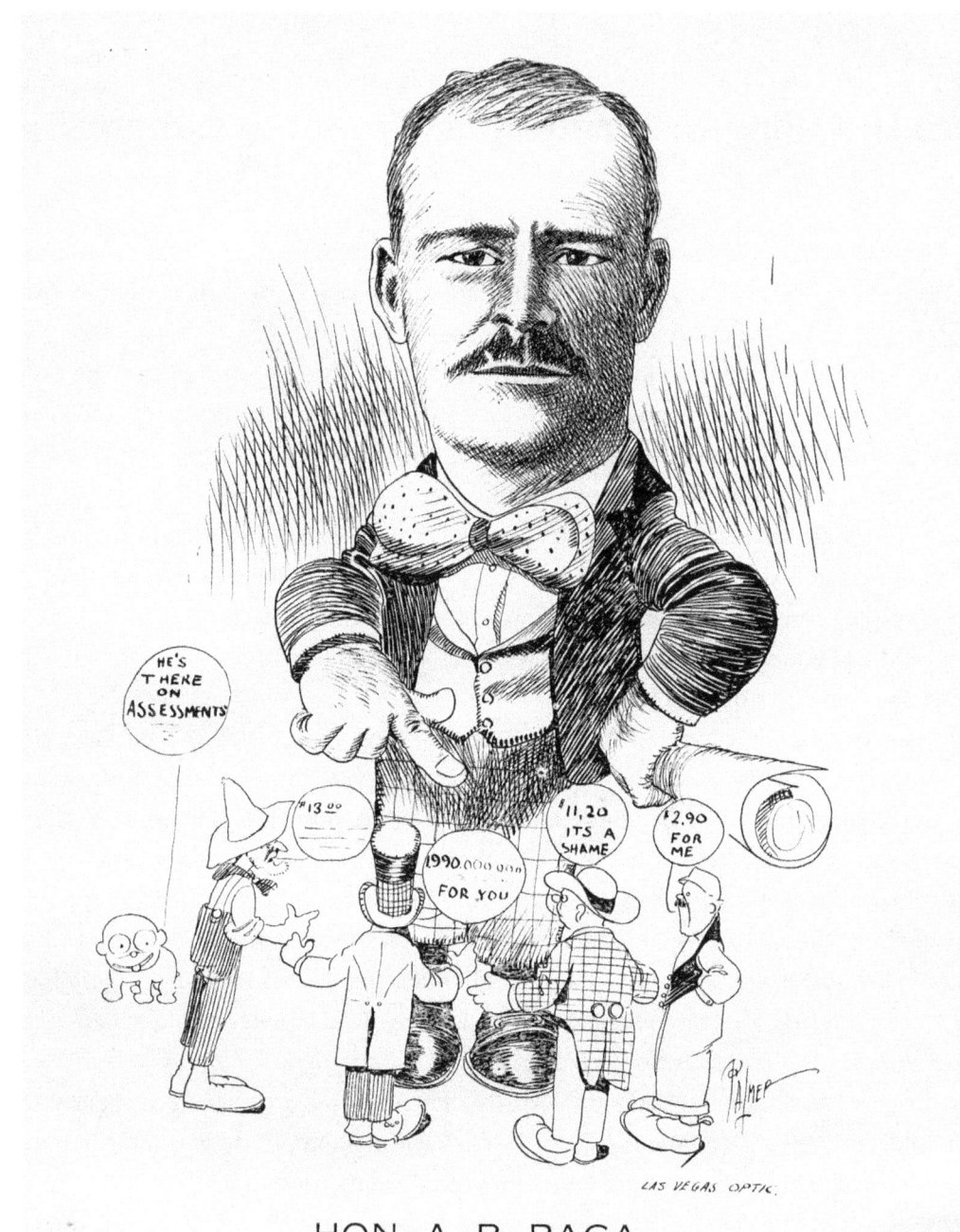

HON. A. B. BACA,
SOCORRO

A.B. Baca: *El otro hermano*

Yes, there was another Baca who was contributing to the social and political fabric of Socorro County when the better known Elfago Baca was occupying the spotlight. It was A.B. (Abdenago) Baca, Elfego's older brother. Findagrave lists his birth date as August 25, 1859. He was born at the now deserted settlement of Tajo near Socorro to Francisco and Juanita Baca. He attended college in Topeka, Kansas.

The two brothers were always close despite their age differences, and Elfego and his family visited A.B. just before Christmas of 1900 when A.B. lived in San Marcial. While he did not possess the notoriety of his younger sibling, A.B. nonetheless exhibited the same law enforcement qualities that had made Elfego famous in the Frisco shootout.

The *Socorro Chieftain* reported one incident in which A.B. was confronted with "two highwaymen" attempting to hold him up around midnight in San Marcial. Baca, then the marshal of Socorro, quickly whipped out his pistol and covered both men, marching them off to jail. It was learned that the two would-be robbers, identified as an "Irishman" and a "Negro," were armed only with a pocket knife between them. Baca declined to press charges, not wishing to put Socorro County to the expense of a trial.

That article alluded to an incident two years earlier when a man murdered a Santa Fe jailer and fled south to Socorro to escape prosecution. Baca captured the killer, identified only by the *Chieftain* as "a Mexican." The escaped murderer was later identified as Jose Telles in an "Act for the Relief" of Baca passed February 28, 1903, by the Territorial Legislature. The bill provided $500 to Baca for Telles's capture, arrest, and return to Santa Fe. Baca's name frequently showed up in the newspapers in connection with law enforcement activities. On November 1, 1906, the *Tucumcari Times* reported that Captain Fred Fornoff of the Territorial Mounted Police requested Baca's services as an interpreter in connection with the apprehension of the accused slayers of two Colorado miners. The two men in custody spoke only Spanish, and Baca was needed to translate their confessions.

Soon, though, Baca transitioned from law enforcement to other branches of public service. In December 1904 he ran a campaign advertisement in the *Chieftain* claiming of himself that "He has already proved that he possesses the qualities of a good Sheriff." In January of 1905 Baca was appointed Socorro County Assessor to succeed John H. Fullerton who resigned after only seventy-seven days in office to become the first captain of the New Mexico Mounted Police. The *History of Fullerton's Rangers* identified Baca as "local political favorite son Abdenago 'A.B.' Baca of San Marcial. (The) former Socorro town marshal, deputy sheriff-jailer and small time rancher...brother of Socorro County District Attorney Elfego Baca."

As assessor, he published annual front-page articles reporting increases in assessed valuation of property to use as a basis for taxation purposes. One, of August 12, 1905, in the *Chieftain* boasted "a substantial increase" over former years. Baca was serving as assessor on January 21, 1911, because records show that he, along with many others, was pressed into service as an election judge in Magdalena for the proposed new state constitution. He was identified as "Assessor."

In the spring of 1913 Baca barely escaped death when an automobile he was driving, with assistant assessor Ellias Baca as passenger, was involved in a roll-over. On May 15 the *El Paso Herald* reported the two men "narrowly escaped being crushed to death" when their Ford's "hind wheel" broke as they were descending a hill twenty-two miles west of Magdalena. Suffering with various broken bones, they were taken to the Wilson Hotel in Magdalena to recuperate until they were strong enough to return to Socorro.

Baca died July 23, 1916, about a month and a half shy of his fifty-seventh birthday. In reporting on his death the *Chieftain* of July 29 commented that "(t)he summons to another world" came as "no surprise" because he "began to succumb to the dread disease cancer of the stomach." "Death must have been a welcome relief..."

Following religious graveside services, the Alianza Hispano-Americana conducted the burial service. The funeral procession was one of the longest in Socorro in many years, wrote the *Chieftain*. A.B. Baca is buried in San Miguel Cemetery in Socorro.

HON. ELFEGO BACA.
SOCORRO

Elfego Baca: The man, the legend. The truth and the maybes

Answer the following questions about Elfego Baca true or false:
1. Was born on a ball field.
2. Was captured by Indians.
3. Shot up a town with Billy the Kid.
4. Fought off eighty cowboys for thirty-three hours, killing four and escaping without a scratch.
5. Made friends with Poncho Villa.
6. Made an enemy of Pancho Villa but lived to tell about it.
7. Represented a foreign revolutionary power in the United States.
8. Was acquitted of Federal perjury charges.
9. Held nearly every elective office in Socorro County and sought nearly every elective office in New Mexico.
10. Died in bed—at age eighty; probably with his boots on.

The answers? True or mostly true. Some say his mother gave birth to him while playing basketball. This could not be true since James Naismith did not invent the sport until 1891; it must have been baseball. The abduction by Indians, if it occurred at all, likely took place when the Baca family was moving from Elfego's birthplace in Socorro to Topeka, Kansas. Baca, along with other officials, was acquitted of perjury charges the Federal government brought in connection with his defense of Mexican Revolutionary General José Ynéz Salazar. The other questions? There is anecdotal evidence to support affirmative answers to most of them. True or not, Baca was larger than life and he preferred it that way.

Baca was a colorful character, a true son of the Old West who never needed a press agent. He was his own one man PR firm. He was in love with his own image and promoted it through deeds and words until his death in Albuquerque in 1945 at age eighty. His legacy lives on in books and magazine articles. Bronze sculptures of him are priced in the thousands of dollars.

What was the single event that catapulted Baca to his lasting legacy? In October of 1884, at age nineteen, Baca appointed himself a deputy of Socorro County and responded to a call to restore order in the small hamlet of Lower San Francisco Plaza (now Reserve) in far Southwestern New Mexico, one hundred miles from his home base of Socorro. Bored cowboys had come into the village, drunk themselves silly, shot it up, and were terrorizing local residents. What Baca did in the next day a half propelled him to lasting notoriety.

The young deputy entered the bar and arrested intoxicated cowboy Charlie McCarty. Baca took the cowhand prisoner and sought refuge in a nearby *jacal* (small adobe house). McCarty's friends attempted a peaceful resolution. But Baca opened fire, killing one of them. The ensuing standoff precipitated a firefight between the deputy and some eighty cowboys with perhaps a thousand rounds expended. The floor of the house where Baca had taken shelter had a slightly recessed dirt floor, and he was thus able to avoid even a single wound. During the siege he had killed four and wounded eight others. Baca emerged unscathed after thirty-three hours. His lasting fame was assured.

Countless interviews magazine articles, two books, a television series, and a movie guaranteed that. In 1936 he told interviewer Janet Smith, who was compiling a WPA oral history project, "I never wanted to kill anybody, but if a man had it in his mind to kill me, I made it my business to get him first." He was full of such bravado, often unnecessary and unverified. He also told Smith of shooting a cowboy in a gun battle and then being asked the victim's name. "I said I didn't know," Baca allegedly replied. "He wasn't able to tell me by the time I caught up with him." He told someone else of his rule for how long he gave himself to capture a miscreant, even a murderer. "Never longer than forty-eight hours." And if his self-imposed deadline was not met? He would write him. "Please give yourself up. If you don't, I'll know you intend to resist arrest and I will feel justified in shooting you on sight." His goal as a lawman? (To have) "the outlaws to hear my steps a block away."

What others said of him is only slightly less memorable. Leon Metz, in *The Shooters*: "He drank too much; talked too much...he had a weakness for wild women. He was often arrogant and, of course, he showed no compunction about killing people." Baca wanted his story told his way. Kyle S. Crichton, who in 1928 wrote *Law and Order, Ltd.: The Rousing Life of Elfego Baca of New Mexico*. "That it (his name) is known only fleetingly elsewhere (besides the Southwest) is no fault of Elfego Baca's." New Mexico born writer Harvey Fergusson called him "a knight-errant from the romantic point of view if ever the six-shooter West produced one." What actions, besides the Frisco shootout, prompted such comments? There were many, often showing a generous persona.

Despite his very macho image which he did his best to project, Baca had a distinctly softer side, especially when it came to fellow Hispanics. While serving as county clerk, he often waived statutory fees at the end of the year, his own form of holiday tax amnesty, knowing that poorer citizens (which often meant his race), would appreciate not having to pay even $5 for some routine assessment normally charged. As school superintendent he awarded premiums to children for outstanding achievement and attendance.

Baca also had a populist leaning. He once erected a new public building in Socorro by arresting "all tramps" and putting them to work, even when those "tramps" were stonemasons, adobe makers, plasterers and the like. (Hamm *New Mexico Magazine*) His "Manifesto" when he ran for New Mexico Governor in 1924 had several planks appealing to the poor voters. Among them were a $200,000 appropriation to build a state hospital to treat and care for the poor, a state appropriation for orphanages instead of forcing them to rely on private donations, and a law creating a public defender's office to represent those charged with a criminal offense who were too poor to employ an attorney.

As did his chroniclers, so did Hollywood love him. In 1958 the Walt Disney Studios produced a miniseries called *The Nine Lives of Elfego Baca* and followed that with a movie entitled *Elfego Baca: Six Gun Law*, released in 1962. The movie was cobbled together from episodes of the series.

Baca was admitted to the New Mexico Bar in 1894 at age twenty nine. He later became deputy federal marshal, assistant district attorney, mayor of Socorro, sheriff of Socorro County, and superintendent of schools. He was frequently called the best sheriff Socorro County ever had.

Mexico figured prominently in Baca's life. During the Mexican Revolution he represented Victoriano Huerta's government in the United States. This earned him an indictment for criminal conspiracy when Mexican general José Inés Salazar escaped from prison at Fort Bliss, Texas, on the border. He was also reputed to have taken a pistol from the angry revolutionary leader Pancho Villa, who allegedly put a $30,000 bounty on his head.

In his declining years, Baca kept an office on Central Avenue in downtown Albuquerque, giving interviews, practicing law, and running for office when he felt like it. As Metz put it: "For years he was a local fixture of controversial pride, an anachronism of another time, a colorful individual whose fires of life still flamed in his droll and witty stories." Elfego Baca died peacefully in bed, an old man.

HON. CHAS. L. BALLARD.
ROSWELL

Charles L. Ballard: Rough Rider, lawman, public servant

Charles L. Ballard is not the only lawman in the *Optic Cartoon Book*, but he is likely the best known. His caricature depicted him not as the Chaves County Sheriff he once was but instead holding a Cattle Sanitary Board sign and a placard depicting him as a Rough Rider and Governor's staff member. All of those things he was but much more.

Ballard was so many things at so many times in his life that perhaps the *Cartoon Book* caricaturist had trouble keeping all Ballard's roles straight. Those included an early association with notorious sheriff Charles C. Perry. Perry's well chronicled disgrace (Ball 1986) never attached to Ballard, however. Ballard's days as a deputy in Eddy County under Perry included chasing and capturing infamous outlaws of the day and breaking up a boxing match in El Paso. (Fleming 1991) There were other famous or infamous personages of the Old West as well whose names surface when Ballard's name is mentioned

He may not have known Billy the Kid as some have claimed. However, he did know the Kid's slayer (Pat Garrett); and Ballard did run an unlicensed gaming house where one well known face at the poker table was that of the famed lawman Pat Garrett. (State Records Center and Archives as reported in *Treasures of History Vol. II*) So it is little wonder that media of Ballard's day was prone to paint a somewhat overblown picture of him.

The *Las Vegas Optic*, in an effusive profile May 26, 1906, included so many flowery comments that one wonders at the account's objectivity. Consider this example: "His modesty, his innate courtesy, his good nature, his winning personality" have made "Charlie Ballard (known) all over the territory." The newspaper also reported that Ballard was a captain in Teddy Roosevelt's Rough Riders. The Troop H mustering out roll shows him discharged as a second lieutenant, the same rank with which he entered. He never left the U.S. for Cuba. He did, however, later serve for a year in the Philippines until illness forced him home. (Fleming and Williams 1991)

This story from the *Optic* may be apocryphal, but it makes for good copy. Ballard did go to the Galapagos Islands for David Goodrich of Goodyear Rubber with whom he had served as a Rough Rider. The mission was to assess the possibility of establishing a cattle ranch there. That venture, however, was cut short by a revolution on the mainland in Ecuador. Returning from South America, Ballard disembarked in New York City en route home. Roosevelt got wind of Ballard's stopover and invited him to the presidential Oyster Bay home. At the end of a pleasant day, so the story goes, Roosevelt insisted on driving Ballard to the train station.

> "How is it, Charlie, that every Rough Rider officer in the regiment and about nine-tenths of the men have asked me for a job, and you have never put in a claim?"
> "Oh. I don't deserve anything and don't want anything," was the response.
> "Well, if there is any place you want that I can give you, it will be necessary only to ask for it."
> "Well, you see, Mr. President, there isn't any job that you can offer me that I would take ...I am a Democrat. If I accepted a position from you people would say I was disloyal to my party, and I would rather remain above suspicion than accept any office in your gift."
> (*Las Vegas Optic*)

Noble sentiments, but accurate? Did this incident even take place? Even the *Las Vegas Optic* noted that "(t)he anecdote, whether true or not, illustrates characteristics that...Ballard unquestionably possesses." In any event, Ballard was one of a forty-man honor guard of former Rough Riders chosen for Roosevelt's inauguration on March 4, 1905. Some accounts even have him commanding the contingent. So he must have enjoyed some close personal association with the President.

That same year, Ballard served one term in the Territorial Senate—the only Democrat in the upper chamber. As Fleming observes, when Herbert J. Hagerman, a fellow Roswell citizen, was appointed Governor, he appointed Ballard to his staff. When George Curry succeeded Hagerman, he too kept Ballard. Returning to Roswell from Santa Fe, Ballard concentrated on resuming his earlier career in law enforcement.

Not done with politics, Ballard ran for sheriff of Chaves County in 1906 and won. That term was marked by his embrace of a radical new technology—the gasoline-powered engine. In March of 1907 he transported a prisoner by bus. Voters must have liked what they saw in this forward-thinking officer of the law. He was elected in 1908 and in 1910. That same year he employed a car to retrieve a prisoner from Plainview, Texas. His time in office was running out, however.

Ballard's last term was only one year and fifteen days because of New Mexico's admission into the Union. The first election under statehood was held in November 1911, and Ballad was turned out of office by Chaves County voters in favor of Clarence R. Young. All new county and state officials assumed office on January 15, 1911. "Charlie Ballard thus served as the last sheriff before statehood," Fleming writes, "and he was very proud of having been one of the last territorial sheriffs."

But when he had put away the badge and pistol for the last time, Ballard remained the person the *Optic* had depicted him as: "a man of ability and determination, of staunch integrity, a brave and capable officer, a hard fighter in the battles of war or peace, and a citizen that all of New Mexico delights to claim."

Thrice married, Ballard died at age eighty-four and was buried in El Paso alongside his first wife.

HON. H. H. BETTS
SILVER CITY

Howard H. Betts: Booster, citizen, leader

"A born booster," the *Las Vegas Optic* wrote in 1906 of Howard H. Betts.

When Betts died sixteen years later, his hometown newspaper, the *Silver City Enterprise*, termed him "one of Silver City and New Mexico's best known citizens." Both accolades were true.

Betts was a hometown promoter by vocation and avocation. For a time he managed the Silver City Chamber of Commerce. In that capacity, the *Enterprise* noted, he published "a splendid booklet" touting the area's resources and attractions to prospective businesses interested in relocating. His business interests, which complemented his promotional activities for his adopted city, included operating a grocery store and engaging in mining and insurance. For several years he was secretary of the Elks lodge and managed its opera house. Business was in his blood. He had found his niche in that pursuit in New York City.

At the age of ten he moved from his native Danbury, Connecticut, to Brooklyn. After high school he went to work with Austin, Nichols & Company, a large wholesale grocery firm. That experience was to stand him in good stead for his first work in Silver City as a retail grocer. Betts knew the grocery business from the ground floor up because that is where he had started—from the bottom as "general utility boy." When he left Austin, Nichols after thirteen years he was running one of its largest departments.

In Silver City when he arrived Christmas Day of 1886 he soon found plenty to keep him occupied, first in the grocery business, and then a short time later as an incorporator of the short-lived Silver City, Pinos Altos, and Mogollon Narrow Gauge Railroad. Such myriad business activities helped lay the foundation for his equally varied community and territorial involvement. He served on the board of regents for the New Mexico Normal School, now Western New Mexico University. On the territorial level Betts served on the Bureau of Immigration (the department of commerce and tourism) and as president of the penitentiary board for two years.

In that capacity he interacted closely with penitentiary superintendent and fellow Republican Holm O. Bursum. Betts was a brother-in-law of William H. Newcomb, who was also included in the *Optic Cartoon Book*.

Of the all the roles he played, however, none likely was more interesting than that, along with his wife, as movie extras in a film shot in 1912 when Silver City was briefly at the center of the movie making business in the United States under the legendary director Romaine Fielding. Here is the way the *Silver City Independent* reported the event in its July 11, 1913, edition: "A number of Silver City people figured in a musical scene, part of a film drama, staged at the Lubin studio…Sunday morning while a thousand people stood grouped around the studio, watching the interesting proceedings. All the ladies appeared in evening dresses and the gentlemen wore dress suits."

Throughout his life, Betts held numerous important positions of trust and responsibility, both as an involved citizen of his community and as an elected official. During World War I he worked with the Red Cross and served as secretary of the local draft board. He was city clerk from 1897 until his death and served two terms as deputy assessor. He was still working in his insurance office the day before his death and was no doubt telling one and all what a fine place Silver City was in which to live and work.

Howard H. Betts: Community booster and good citizen.

C. N. BLACKWELL,
RATON

Christopher N. Blackwell: A Confederate New Mexican

Christopher N. Blackwell was born April 20, 1847, in Carroll County in the border state of Missouri. As a sympathizer to the Southern cause, he joined the Conference forces as a teenager after a brief common school education. At war's end, like so many of his Rebel comrades at arms who saw no future in the South, he headed west. For Blackwell it meant Kit Carson, Colorado, and employment with the wholesale and forwarding firm of Chick & Browne. Some sources show the name as Chick, Browne, and Co. When the company was succeeded by Browne and Manzanares he was sent to its new headquarters in Socorro in 1879.

New Mexico opened new vistas and was to be his home the rest of his life. Blackwell entered banking after twenty years with Browne and Manzanares, advancing to the position of vice president. But he soon found himself launching new financial institutions in the northern part of the territory. He helped organize the San Miguel National Bank in Las Vegas and in 1892 played a similar role with the First National Bank of Raton taking the post of cashier. He remained there until his death. Banking led to new opportunities in the coal-rich Colfax area of New Mexico, and he was to play a major role in developing the north central area of the state.

Aside from his business obligations, Blackwell also participated actively in Masonic affairs. He had been initiated into the order in Missouri and was eager to bring the order to New Mexico. He organized a chapter in Socorro while working for Browne and Manzanares and served as treasurer of a new chapter in Raton. But coal and its possibilities beckoned.

The story is best told by Ronald E. Bromley in *The Last Train to Leave Cimarron, New Mexico: Why the Trains Left*. The Raton area had plenty of coal. Not all of the territory did, however. Blackwell and others, including investors from St. Louis, envisioned new markets for coal and coke if only there were a way to transport the coal. The solution, as they saw it, was to build a new railroad. Accordingly they filed for incorporation, capitalized at $1,000,000, and issued stock. The St. Louis, Rocky Mountain and Pacific Railroad Company was up and rolling. The investors also owned the Rocky Mountain and Pacific Company with major land holdings in the north central part of the territory. Major holdings indeed: The company owned 191,895 acres of coal rich lands near Raton and mineral rights to another 328,430. The proposed route was from Des Moines, New Mexico, through Raton and various smaller communities, and to the Taos Valley.

Blackwell died April 7, 1934. He had accomplished big things for a Southern boy who had started life on a poor Missouri farm.

F. O. BLOOD, ESQ.,
LAS VEGAS

F.O. Blood: From barkeep to mayor

Saloon and billiard hall owner, miner, railroader, football team manager, New Mexico state representative, postmaster, and mayor: When F.O. Blood died in Las Vegas in 1929 he had done all those things. Born in Westport, New York, in 1859, Blood moved to Kansas as a youth. There he went to work for the Atchison, Topeka, and Santa Fe Railroad. After three years he quit to follow mining in White Oaks, New Mexico. In that city he also opened a saloon and billiard hall. But railroading was in his blood.

He returned to Topeka to rejoin the Santa Fe but was transferred to San Marcial, New Mexico, as a storekeeper. In 1896 he was promoted to division storekeeper in Las Vegas with responsibilities for that portion of the line extending from La Junta, Colorado, to El Paso. He remained in Las Vegas the rest of his busy life but somehow found time to organize the Las Vegas Tigers football team in 1900.

Blood remained with the Santa Fe until his appointment as postmaster of East Las Vegas on March 14, 1902, by President William McKinley. He was reappointed two years later. The *Las Vegas Optic* called him "progressive" and "public spirited" and added that his loyalty to the Republican Party was "one of the things on which he most prides himself."

He entered politics and in 1911 worked with Territorial Representative William H. Andrews in the push for statehood and oversaw election preparations in his city. In 1915 he served in the New Mexico House of Representatives and served on several committees, including public printing, privileges and elections, and disbursement of public moneys.

A few years later he turned his sights to local politics and was elected mayor of East Las Vegas. He headed a ticket which was reelected in a close race in April of 1929. Seven years later he would be dead at age seventy.

WALTER S. BOWEN, Esq.,
ALBUQUERQUE

Walter S. Bowen: Insurance Man

Walter S. Bowen was an insurance man much of his professional life. A native of Ohio, Bowen as a teenager left the farm where he was born. At seventeen he began making and selling farm machinery. In 1883 he ran a clay products plant in Tacoma, Washington, with a work force of 200. He oversaw that operation fourteen years. The year 1901 saw him join the Equitable Life Assurance Society, an association he maintained for more than a quarter of a century.

In his new home of Portland, Oregon, Bowen quickly became one of Equitable's leading personal underwriters of life insurance in the Pacific Northwest. In recognition of his achievements the company offered him the management of the Albuquerque agency. In his first year in New Mexico, Bowen doubled the office's 1904 productivity.

He accomplished that despite a general stagnation in the insurance business and an investigation of the insurance industry by a legislative committee in New York State where many of the country's leading insurance companies were headquartered. The investigation's results, contained in the Armstrong Report and denounced by some in the industry as "radical," called for wide-ranging reforms. The report targeted the so-called "Big Three"—the Equitable, Mutual, and New York Life. The *New York Times* reported that experts said it struck "at the very root" of the insurance business. Nonetheless, Bowen's outstanding record in Albuquerque resulted in the Society expanding his sales territory to include Arizona, much of southwest Texas, and the Mexican states of Sonora and Chihuahua.

The *Albuquerque Morning Journal* reported on his business activities in its January 20, 1925, edition, and the *Marion (Iowa) Sentinel* carried similar news in September 9, 1926.

H. D. BOWMAN, ESQ.,
LAS CRUCES

Henry D. Bowman: Banker, area booster

Henry D. Bowman developed his banking skills and business acumen at an early age. Born in Minneapolis in 1860, Bowman and his father and brothers came west and bought their first bank in Las Cruces when he was just twenty-three. By 1903 he was the sole owner. Bowman's bank was reorganized as the Bowman Bank and Trust seven years later. Continued acquisitions of related financial institutions followed rapidly.

He soon became president of the Southwestern Abstract & Title Company and treasurer of the Las Cruces Building & Improvement Company and the South & West Land & Development Company. By 1921 the Bowman Bank and Boyd Union Bank, both struggling, merged as Bowman's Bank and Trust Company, but the firm failed the following year.

Bowman did not have formal training in business. He had attended the University of Michigan Medical Department but did not take a degree.

Despite heavy business commitments, Bowman took active roles in politics and projects to improve southern New Mexico. He was a member of the Republican State Central Committee and was treasurer of the Elephant Butte Water Users Association.

He died the day after Thanksgiving, 1934.

C. T. BROWN, ESQ.,
SOCORRO

Cony T. (C.T.) Brown: A "most capable" mining man; School of Mines benefactor

Ralph Emerson Twitchell was spot on in calling Cony T. (C.T.) Brown "one of the most capable mining men" in the Southwest. "Few, ..." he noted in *Leading Facts of New Mexican History*, "have taken a more helpful part" in developing New Mexico's mineral resources. Twitchell's accolades also encompassed Brown's crucial role in the early years of the New Mexico School of Mines. Robert W. Eveleth, in a biography of Brown, writes this: "Brown is perhaps best remembered for his unfailing devotion to, and support of, the New Mexico School of Mines." His early years, however, were hardly preparation for the recognition and praise to be heaped on him and for such an illustrious, productive career.

After obtaining a secondary education at the Maine Central Institute, an independent college preparatory school in his native state, Brown moved west to Kansas to farm and to work in the hardware business. In 1880 he moved even further west—this time to New Mexico—where at age twenty-four he discovered mining. It was to become a lifelong vocation. A lack of formal professional education proved no obstacle to this energetic and enterprising young man. His first employment in the industry was as superintendent of the Ellis Mining Company's Magdalena district mine. He was later a district manager for the Empire Zinc Company's properties in Grant County. Not content with just one foot in the profession, Brown was also an independent operator and lessor. Those interests and activities must have seemed endless.

His travel must have seemed endless as well. As an ore buyer and expert examiner for Empire Zinc, he routinely visited the company's properties in Mexico. The pursuit of personal mining interests also meant travel from one end of the United States to the other and to Canada and Central America. In the field "Captain Brown" (as he was known to associates in Mexico and north of the border) must have presented "quite the dashing figure with his tall frame decked out in leather lace-up boots, khakis, long-billed cap, and field pouch." (Eveleth) Meanwhile, back in Socorro, Brown's wife, the daughter of a former Prussian army surgeon and likely accustomed as a girl to her father's comings and goings, took it in stride. Her husband was peripatetic. Unfortunately, Brown's hectic schedule of travel, business interests, and public and political service took it's collective toll.

Brown is said to have returned home to Socorro on Christmas morning after three weeks away, remarking that he might "stay at home long enough to get acquainted with his neighbors." (Reynolds 1997) As it turned out, he did not have time. His death on January 15, 1925, occurred as he was preparing for still another trip—this time to Santa Fe to participate in a session of the legislature. Eveleth writes that Brown had returned home with "a terrible cold that...quickly deteriorated into pneumonia." Brown had not planned to allow a cold, even a bad one, to deter him from his public duties if he could help it.

Always an active Republican, he had served on the Socorro City Council twelve years and had chaired the Socorro County Board of County Commissioners. In addition to his service in Santa Fe as a state senator, Brown also chaired the Middle Rio Grande Reclamation Association. Notwithstanding his heavy public involvement, he channeled his considerable energies into several entrepreneurial endeavors.

Those led him into varied pursuits, such as Socorro agent for a coal company, a buggy company, and a bicycle outlet. He was president of the Socorro State Bank, president and manager of the Socorro Power and Light Company, and president of the historic Val Verde Hotel. But not every endeavor met with success. He was an incorporator of the Black Range Railway to serve that mining district. The railway was one of the few of his endeavors that failed to materialize. Service to the mining industry, however, continued to bring him repeated recognition. He was frequently a delegate to the International Mining Congress and in 1920 joined in organizing the New Mexico Mining Association, precursor to the New Mexico Chapter of the American Mining Congress. He was on its first board of directors.

However, Brown's abiding interest was in his hometown's mining school. There was no better champion, no better source of encouragement or support when dark times loomed over the young New Mexico School of Mines (now the New Mexico Institute of Mining and Technology) after it opened in 1889. Calling him a "figure of near legendary proportions," Eveleth bemoans

Brown's relative lack of contemporary recognition on campus. Except for a short article in the school's newspaper in 1925, the record provides little on Brown's early involvement with the institution. Despite its brevity, the article is illuminating because it offers this insight: "It was largely due to his (Brown's) efforts that the school was started and maintained."

Those efforts took many avenues. Brown served on the school's board of trustees as secretary-treasurer from 1889 until 1914 and again from 1914 until 1921 when he was elected president. In addition, he frequently helped secure important donations of laboratory equipment and often used his near limitless contacts to help graduates find jobs and then advance in their careers. Reportedly he assisted the school with large sums of money when financial woes threatened. In 1914 the school recognized him with its first honorary degree. A campus building bears his name.

Cony T. Brown: Capable mining man, important figure to the School of Mines.

WILLIAM A. BUDDECKE, Esq.,
LAS VEGAS

William A. Buddecke: Utility executive

Before moving from his native Missouri to Las Vegas for his wife's health, William A. Buddecke was a stockholder and manager of the St. Louis branch of the Johns Manville Company. At the time his caricature appeared in the *Las Vegas Optic* on February 20, 1906, he was president of the Las Vegas Railway and Power Company. During an excursion on his line two days later to Las Vegas area scenic attractions with Governor Herbert J. Hagerman and other dignitaries the car in which they were riding jumped the tracks and was involved in a serious accident. Buddecke was thrown out and suffered a badly broken leg and a gashed head. The results of the injuries remained with him the rest of his life.

Buddecke was always alert for possibilities to invest in other utilities and to assist other New Mexico cities in similar undertakings. In late 1905 his company acquired Las Vegas Light and Fuel Company and in April of 1906 he bought the interests of secretary and treasurer H. G. Dammer. He also worked with Holm O. Bursum to install an electric light plant in Socorro and with landowner and capitalist J.D. Hand on a similar undertaking in Mora.

In addition to his business activities, which included serving as president of the Point Milling and Mining Company of Mineral Point, Missouri, Buddecke was also a director of the Las Vegas Commercial Club and secretary of the Fair and Fall Festival.

HON. WM. B. BUNKER,
LAS VEGAS

William B. Bunker: Attorney, public servant

William B. Bunker came to Las Vegas from Indiana in 1886 having studied law and earning a degree from Purdue University. He immediately immersed himself in the legal profession in his new home town. He soon was named deputy clerk and in November of 1888 was appointed clerk of the United States Court. Upon expiration of his term Bunker entered private practice.

An ardent Democrat, he was elected to the New Mexico Territorial Senate and later served three terms as Las Vegas City Attorney. He was a member of the City Commission and on the territorial level was president of the Board of Immigration. Bunker also served as a United States Commissioner.

He was active in positions of leadership with the Elks lodge.

Bunker died October 2, 1932, in Oakland, California at age sixty-nine.

HON. H. O. BURSUM,
SOCORRO

Holm O. Bursum: A Horatio Alger figure of the Old West

Holm O. Bursum was a figure straight out of Horatio Alger's novels. The nineteenth century American writer was known for his tales of impoverished boys and their rise from humble backgrounds to achieving success and contributing to society. That was Holm O. Bursum. His story must have cried out to James Graham McNary for inclusion in the *Optic Cartoon Book*. Born in Fort Dodge, Iowa, on February 10, 1867, to Norwegian immigrants Frank and Maria (Hilton) Bursum, young Holm was orphaned at age twelve. As a tough resilient youth with a great deal of native intelligence, he acquired only a few years of formal education in the Fort Dodge public schools before landing in Colorado Springs where he supported himself as best he could at minimum wage jobs in drug stores and restaurants. In 1882 he made his way to San Antonio, New Mexico. In that tiny village just south of Socorro his life took an upward lasting turn—to one of success and achievement.

In San Antonio he joined Uncle Gus Hilton clerking in Hilton's general merchandise store. Cousin Conrad and son of Gus, later to achieve fame as an international hotelier, was a close friend and fellow employee. The two were to remain firm friends the rest of their lives. Everyone in the territory called the newcomer simply "Bursum," even his wife. Hilton was an exception. He called him "Olaf," using Bursum's middle name.

But the newcomer from Colorado found working for himself more to his liking. A few years later he negotiated a U.S. government contract to haul supplies to the Army at Fort Wingate in western New Mexico. There he also dabbled in horse trading but found it unprofitable because the Navajos he encountered would steal from him at night the horses they had sold to him during the day. After four years of hard work he had amassed enough capital—twenty-eight mules and a few wagons—to allow him to return to the Socorro area.

He later traded that for a sheep ranch, his first. One asset, without price and one which he had acquired along the way, was to stand him in good stead the rest of his career. It was a fluency in Spanish, the *lingua franca* of territorial New Mexico. But it was never business or the pursuit of commercial enterprise that fascinated Bursum. It was politics—of the Republican leaning.

In 1894 he won his first elective race as sheriff of Socorro County. Bursum had found his true lasting vocation. As the *Las Vegas Optic* was to later note, "He has never been too much engrossed in his business life to not give a large measure of time and interest to political affairs." The newspaper went on to observe that "He has always been a zealous Republican."

In 1898 he found another lifelong love. He married Lulu M. Moore of Silver City, whom he had met at a country dance. Together they had four children. Son Holm Jr. was to follow him into politics, most notably as a longtime mayor of Socorro. Politics was in the elder Bursum's blood, and it would remain so until the end of his days. It was also in the DNA of Holm Jr., Holm III, and Holm IV.

Today "rising star" is perhaps an overworked metaphor to mark a newcomer's ascendancy in politics. It was not in Bursum's case. Several things came in quick succession in those heady years of the early 1900s. He met Governor Miguel A. Otero, who was to become his patron; he was elected Chairman of the Territorial Republican Central Committee (1905-1911); he began the first of seven terms as a delegate to the Republican National Convention (1904-1928); and he was a delegate to the New Mexico Territorial Constitutional Convention (1910).

All of this service in the first decade of the new century prepared him, along with other prominent New Mexicans of the day, to make the successful push for statehood in 1912. His extensive letter writing campaigns, his numerous visits around the territory, his strong personal appeals, and his countless visits to Washington—all at his own expense—had the desired effect. President William Howard Taft signed the statehood bill on January 6, 1912. Bursum's role cannot be overestimated.

Bursum in 1906 concluded seven-years as superintendent of the New Mexico Territorial Penitentiary, a post to which Otero had appointed him. After leaving territorial service in Santa Fe he returned to Socorro where he spent the next few years in active ranch management and in improving his cash flow.

But he could never stay out of politics very long; the call could not be resisted. In 1911 and 1916, he made two runs for governor. He was, of course, the Republican candidate in the first gubernatorial contest under statehood. Bursum had many memorable moments. In a prophetic aside, he told delegates to the 1911 Las Vegas convention that "the results of this election can hardly be estimated. It will in a measure settle the future politics of this state." (Hamm 2012) His election plank was a model for others to emulate. He called for a need for the new state to operate on a cash basis, the need for public education, and the rights of workers to be safe in their workplace.

"You can always know where to find him," John E. Griffith told his fellow delegates in the wind-up to the nominating speech. Griffith, the district attorney from Socorro County, had been given the honor of nominating Bursum. "He fights fair and in the open. He is not a bush-whacker. You can call him up at any hour of the day or night and at once find out how he stands on any topic....he will stand like a stone wall or the Rock of Ages for all to see for what he believes is right...." (Griffith 1911) But the governorship was not to be, even after two tries.

On March 11, 1921, Governor Merritt C. Mechem appointed Bursum to the U.S. Senate seat vacated by Albert B. Fall when Fall became Secretary of the Interior. Bursum then won the special election in September of 1921 over Richard Hanna to fill out the balance of Fall's term. It was a bigger prize as it was on the national stage and gave him an opportunity to make his contributions for the entire country, not just for New Mexico. And he quickly did. It was during this term that his work for veterans as chairman of the Senate Pensions Committee attracted national attention. Despite his many contributions in Washington, however, he could not retain his Senate seat. In 1924 he lost to Judge Sam Bratton in the 1924 U.S. Senate contest in a bitterly challenged outcome. Two years later he left public service for good.

Bursum achieved many milestones in his long life. Among them were his service in the Senate, election to his first public office at twenty-eight, attendance at seven Republican National Conventions, service as Superintendent of the Territorial Penitentiary, service as a delegate to the New Mexico Territorial Constitutional Convention, tenure as mayor of Socorro, service on the Republican National Committee, chairmanship of the Territorial Republican

Central Committee, important service to American veterans, and his important role in gaining statehood for New Mexico.

His outstanding personal hallmarks were part of his fabric. He was the ultimate party loyalist. He did everything in his power to mend fences and even support those who had betrayed him. As penitentiary superintendent he took it as a personal affront when a prisoner escaped and did everything in his power to return the escapee to custody. He was never down for long, but when he was he remembered this: "When times are tough and you are out of money, you put on a clean white shirt, spruce up, and get out there and go to work." (Hamm 2012)

But his aging body began to betray him. He had done all he could do for his party, his state, and his country. Death came for him in a Colorado Springs nursing home on August 7, 1953. The Socorro *El Defensor* got it exactly right in reporting on his death: It said his "outstanding ability and knowledge of the industrial, social, and economic problems of New Mexico were largely formulated through frontier experiences." He was schooled in what it took to advance and it was enough. The one-time restaurant waiter, general store clerk, freighter, railroad hand, horse trader, rancher, home town mayor, party leader, public servant for his state and country, husband to Lulu and father to Claire, Ruth Mildred, Holm Otto Junior, and Betty Kathryn could do no more.

E. A. CAHOON, ESQ.,
ROSWELL

Edward A. Cahoon: A moving force in growth of the Pecos Valley

The story behind Roswell's Cahoon Park, as told by Elis Fleming and Ernestine Williams, is interesting because the park once served as a way stop during the Depression for Oklahoma families fleeing the Dust Bowl for a new start in California. Once called Haynes' Dream, the park now honors Edward A. Cahoon—one of Roswell's best known citizens and a pioneer developer of southeast New Mexico. Despite the park's original name, transients were not encouraged to stay because local people feared they might compete for jobs. This is interesting but not nearly as much as Cahoon's story.

Anyone daring and far-sighted enough to dream of starting a bank in 1890 when there were barely 500 people in all of Chaves County and then making sure that vaults and other needed equipment were freighted by wagon 200 miles from Albuquerque to Roswell makes for a compelling story. That just begins to tell Edward Cahoon's story as laid out by Georgia Redfield.

Cahoon may have had only a few years of banking experience in Albuquerque before starting a new life in Roswell, but he had the necessary requisites—a prestigious Eastern college degree and three years of toughening him up for anything life might throw at him as a cowboy on a 50,000 acre spread near Cimarron.

How he came to the cowboying life is an unusual one for a New Englander. After growing up in Vermont, he graduated from one of the best schools in the east, Amherst College. The year 1884 found him in Minneapolis working at real estate where an acquaintance told him of great opportunities in New Mexico. That was enough for a young man eager to make his mark in a new land. Three years in the saddle, enjoyable and life forming as they were, were plenty. In 1887 Cahoon accepted a clerking position with the First National Bank of Albuquerque. Little did he know he was to remain in banking the remainder of his life.

Accepting an invitation from local merchants needing a hometown bank, Cahoon helped organize the Bank of Roswell. It opened July 26, 1890. There he remained for the next forty-four years. Cahoon was now perfectly positioned to aid the area by supporting business enterprises through financing farms, ranches, and homes—all the bedrock of a strong community. Cahoon and Roswell were a perfect fit in both his professional and public life.

He did make one venture outside banking, which ultimately supported Roswell and Chaves County in another way—by linking them to the outside world. *Treasures of History IV*, a Chaves County Historical Society publication, relates that in May of 1894 Cahoon and John W. Poe teamed up to launch the Pioneer Telephone & Manufacturing Co. Cahoon came aboard the fledgling business as treasurer while Poe completed the management team as president. Poe had been Pat Garrett's deputy the night his boss shot and killed Billy the Kid at Fort Sumner. The initial venture into the telephone business proved unsuccessful, but, undaunted, in 1894 the two organized the Roswell Telephone and Manufacturing Co. That effort brought the first telephones to Roswell. Cahoon had exhibited the grit and determination to make a go of whatever he undertook, even if it took a few years and a second try.

President of the New Mexico Bankers Association, president of the Roswell Commercial Club—the roll call goes on and on. Satisfying as it was, professional attainment was not enough. That was to become the springboard for Cahoon's public and charitable work, such as assisting deserving youth and helping many of them to obtain college educations.

Cahoon was a leading figure in founding and building the New Mexico Military Institute, a signature educational achievement for both him and for Roswell. His contributions to NMMI were marked by naming the Cahoon Armory for him. During the Depression he quietly assisted struggling families and helped young people attain a higher education. When he died at age seventy-two two days before Christmas 1934, Cahoon had built a record of achievement and service to his community that is still recognized today.

COLONEL MAX FROST,
SANTA FE

Max Frost: Journalist, power broker

When Max Frost died October 13, 1909, the *Santa Fe New Mexican* headlined his death "Leader in Journalism, Politics, Masonry...Left His Imprint Upon History of Southwest... Career Crowded With Work and Achievements." The view a century later is quite the opposite. "Max Frost, soldier, lawyer, political broker and protector of the (Santa Fe) Ring..." is the assessment offered by Robert K. Dean. The Ring was a group of attorneys, politicians, party insiders, and others who gained wealth and influence through corruption, intimidation, and fraudulent land deals. Howard R. Lamar called Frost "a spokesman" for the Ring, perhaps one of the lesser charges leveled at him.

Frost owned the *New Mexican* so the newspaper's fawning was to be expected. His Republican Party cronies with whom he consorted and connived for decades to run New Mexico also lamented his passing. Dean expands on his charges at length in "King Maker in the Back Room, Editor Max Frost, 1876–1909." His article is the basis for much of this profile. It is not a flattering portrayal. In life, Frost had both admirers and detractors. In death, his critics' views prevail.

Contemporary views are a good starting place even if they are sometimes overly servile. Frost, the *New Mexican* continued in its obituary, "was a bundle of restless energy and ambition that leaped over obstacles that would have daunted the strongest of men." It was the "ambition" dimension that concerned the *New York Times*. The newspaper, an implacable foe and unrelenting critic, saw Frost much differently. On December 1, 1908, it called him the "undisputed Republican dictator of New Mexico." He was until President Theodore Roosevelt's appointment of Herbert J. Hagerman as governor broke Frost's grip on the New Mexico Republican Party. Papers as far afield as the Midwest took notice. The *Stevens Point Journal* in Wisconsin concurred with the *Times*, calling Frost "the power behind the throne" in Santa Fe.

What was it that set their journalistic teeth on edge? It was the lust for land. The *Times'* indignation could be traced to the many land grabs in New Mexico it had investigated. Many were orchestrated by the Santa Fe Ring in whose participation Frost was often a willing participant. Frost's involvement with the Ring predated and continued during his ownership of the *New Mexican*.

But it was not just newspapers who were outraged. Former Governor Miguel A. Otero vented his anger many years later charging that New Mexico had been "dominated by one of the most corrupt, unscrupulous, and daring organizations ever connected with its history." Otero knew of what he spoke; the Ring had stolen his family's land. That was one charge that could not be leveled at Frost.

His appearance on the Santa Fe stage did not even begin as a civilian. Frost came to New Mexico as a young Army telegrapher in 1876 with the U.S. Army Signal Corps to build a military telegraph line in New Mexico and into eastern Arizona and as far as Fort Stockton, Texas. It was vital work. The *Las Vegas Optic* said the telegraph lines "were as important to that section as...railroads" were to be later. Frost soon became so proficient at his task that native folk would refer to him as "the man who made the wires talk."

The young soldier's military assignment proved fortuitous because it afforded him an opportunity to rub elbows with newspaper reporters who transmitted their articles over his wires. That connection led to civilian work as a free-lance newspaper correspondent, including the *New Mexican*. *History of New Mexico* gives his association with the *New Mexican* beginning first as a correspondent May 1, 1876, and then in a reportorial and editorial capacity. With ownership came even more power. But that was in the future.

None of it would have come about had a young Maximilian Frost not lied about his age to join the Army in Brooklyn two years after the Civil War ended at Appomattox. But he had climbed the ranks and was a sergeant when he came west. Frost also equivocated about his birthplace. He would say it was New Orleans one time, Vienna another. Maybe he was already showing signs of elusiveness. Years later it would be worse; he would be labeled domineering and manipulative. Lamar writes that as Frost gained power and influence he was "so arrogant and opinionated" that he was disliked even by fellow Republicans. Dean says it was difficult to distinguish where persuasion stopped and bullying began.

Dean sums up the good, the bad, and the ugly in Frost this way: "He was a man of many talents and good deeds, but he too often crossed the line. His desire for personal gain tainted his public service. His pragmatism was so expansive that it accommodated corruption." Few, however, could doubt Frost's love of Santa Fe and New Mexico. He was treasurer of the New Mexico Historical Society and raised funds for a public library. The *New Mexican* observed that "There was no movement for the public good to which he did not contribute in money, time and influence." But philanthropy aside, Frost could be "petty, vindictive, and caustic" when going after his and his party's enemies, notes Dean. When Frost hung up his sergeant's uniform (he was to later exchange it for one of much higher rank), his life changed dramatically.

He began work for the Surveyor General of New Mexico as a deputy surveyor. During this period he gained admission to the bar, specializing in land claims. He learned just how vulnerable the old Spanish land grants were to penetration and manipulation by those who would use the system for their own gain. It was too easy. Temptation beckoned. Frost was indicted.

There are different views of what happened when Frost came before the courts on charges of his role in land fraud. Ralph Emerson Twitchell in *Leading Facts of New Mexican History* provides one view. Lamar in *The Far Southwest* offers another. During President Grover Cleveland's first administration the President directed former Indiana Congressman George W. Julian, "a fearless and incorruptible" public lands expert, to exert "every effort possible...for the purpose of convicting him (Frost) of complicity in land frauds." The government failed, wrote Twitchell. Frost was tried and convicted but won a new trial under Chief Justice Reuben A. Reeves. There he was acquitted.

Even though the Ring's power was in decline, Julian and the *Times* fulminated even more. In 1887 Julian charged in the *North American Review* that the Ring had "hovered over the territory like a pestilence," stealing millions and millions of acres of public land. He claimed the Ring had "dominated governors, judges, district attorneys, legislatures, surveyors-general...and the controlling business interests of the people." His condemnation knew no boundaries. His report was peppered with charges like "organized roguery," "theft of the national patrimony," and "legalized spoliation." The *New York Times* had beaten him to the punch. Three years earlier the newspaper had headlined an article "New-Mexico's Land Ring: Gigantic Swindles Accomplished in the Territory."

Frost's various government positions, including secretary of the Bureau of Immigration (forerunner of the today's tourist office) and his fraternal affiliations, afforded him an entrée to the "instruments of commerce," writes Dean. During Frost's twelve years with the Bureau it circulated "tons of propaganda" and expended untold sums to interest settlers in coming to New Mexico. Marion Dargan says in *The Fight for Statehood* that Governor Herbert J. Hagerman felt the railroads could have spent that $60,000 themselves to increase their businesses rather than having the territory do so. But even Hagerman could not deny that Frost was "a master of the art of propaganda." Perhaps Dargan recalled publications Frost wrote or edited extolling New Mexico's virtues, which included *New Mexico: Its Resources, Climates, Geography*, or another aimed at health-seekers called *How I Cured Myself of Consumption in New Mexico*. Not all of Frost's activities at the Bureau were so benign. Dargan charged that Frost organized "a secret press bureau" to influence smaller weekly newspapers to write favorably of legislation in which the railroads or corporations were interested, sometimes sending them checks of $10 or $100. Frost had long been accustomed to such Machiavellian machinations.

When Frost acquired the *New Mexican* in 1883 "his editor's role strengthened his voice," because "(a) newspaper can take the voice of one, amplify it, and turn it into a roar," notes Dean. Frost owned the newspaper twice, once leasing it to Democrats when his party was out of power, then reacquiring it when the Republicans were back in. Frost was also New Mexico Adjutant General during his ownership and was a colonel in the militia. Under Governor Lew Wallace he helped clear the San Juan area of cattle rustlers and renegade Navajos and Utes. He was one of the few men in the *Optic Cartoon Book* who could legitimately claim the title of "colonel." For most of the others it was merely an honorific bestowed upon them by the head of their party as a friendly gesture to personal friends or political allies. One key adjunct to Frost's professional life was his active association with the Masonic lodge. In this he was not alone.

Many of the non-Hispanics in the *Optic Cartoon Book* were Masons or Elks or both. They likely relied on such memberships to provide vital links to business opportunities or to advance their careers. Frost's prominence with the Masons was such that when he attained the 33rd degree, a rank seldom attained, the *Socorro Chieftain* ran a front page article with a photograph. The *New Mexican* was later to comment that it was in Masonic circles that Frost made "many of his staunchest and most loyal friends."

Frost earned his colonelcy in the territorial militia serving from 1882 until 1886. Likewise, he attained many other positions of leadership and service, including twenty five years on the Republican Central Committee, twelve of them as secretary. Although he had turned the *New Mexican* into "an organ wholly devoted to achieving statehood," notes Dean, it was a goal he did not live to see. Just as Frost's character had changed with assumption of power so did it diminish as the ravages of infirmity overtook him.

Over time, he suffered loss of eyesight, his teeth, control over bodily functions, and mobility. The *Times*, not neglecting an opportunity to cast Frost in an unflattering light, never let up, even in his illness. A dispatch dated November 30, 1906, was headlined "Shouting, Broke His Jaw. Queer Accident to Col. Max Frost, Blind Editor of Santa Fe." The story recounted that Frost, alone in his office on Thanksgiving Day, fractured his jaw yelling for his office boy. When the telephone rang, Frost could not find it and became angered. "Boy," he shouted. But the boy was home eating turkey. "The Colonel's yells grew louder, when suddenly his false teeth fell out, and his jaws came together with such a snap that the jawbone was fractured," the newspaper reported. Frost had suffered a compound fracture; his jaw was put in a cast.

When the end came it came quickly. Frost had worked his entire professional and political life for statehood. But as the momentous event approached, he was too ill to see it achieved. He sold the newspaper in 1909 and spent the last several months of his life in a Kansas City sanitarium. He came home only to die. It was an inglorious decline and an end for a once proud, powerful man.

HON. W. H. GREER,
ALBUQUERQUE

William H. Greer: Stockman, animal rights advocate, showman, streetcar man

He ran one of the biggest ranching operations in New Mexico, earning his stockholders' plaudits for "exceptionally successful and satisfactory" performance. But William H. Greer had an unusual encore to that profession. As a legislator, he later introduced a bill prohibiting steer roping. Perhaps he had seen too much of it; now he perhaps considered it as cruelty to animals disguised as entertainment. Ironically the sport is now a featured event at the state fair he once presided over. Somehow Greer found time to operate the Albuquerque streetcar system as well. Not a man for all seasons but close enough.

As a younger man Greer seemed to be frequently on the move pursuing the "main chance." He did take time out in 1899 to marry Mary Jastro of Bakersfield, California, daughter of the well-known capitalist H.A. Jastro. Greer, a University of Southern California and University of Chicago Law School graduate, made New Mexico his home before finally moving to New York City. There, reported the *Albuquerque Morning Journal*, he died September 23, 1910. He was seventy-two.

Greer followed diverse activities, practicing law in Chicago and working as a stockman and miner in Arizona before locating to New Mexico Territory. Upon moving to Albuquerque after managing the Victoria Land & Cattle Company, he was president of the New Mexico Fair Association, a hugely popular event but from which steer roping was notably absent. David Myric, in *New Mexico's Railroads*, relates the story of Greer's venture into electric cars. According to Myric, Greer also found time in 1903 to organize and serve as president of the Albuquerque Traction Company, the city's first electric car line. Never financially successful, the four-car operation nonetheless did replace horse drawn cars and must have been a source of great civic pride. The city sanitation workers must have liked it too. Horse manure from the transit line was no longer a problem for them. The line ran from Old Town to the newer part of the city three miles away. (Myric 1990) In addition to his business pursuits, the Republican

Party ("a staunch and loyal supporter of its principles") was always a big part of Greer's life.

Ralph Emerson Twitchell, whose *Leading Facts of New Mexican History* provides so many important facts about the *Las Vegas Optic's* subjects, reported that Greer served in the 23rd Territorial Legislature where he not only successfully introduced the steer roping exhibition prohibition measure but a Mounted Police bill as well to enhance public safety. The *Optic* termed him "a hard working and painstaking legislator." He served four years on the New Mexico Central Committee and was an alternate at the 1904 National Republican Convention in Chicago.

William H. Greer: A successful entrepreneur.

JOHN E. GRIFFITH, ESQ.,
SOCORRO

John E. Griffith: Lawyer, orator, political confidant of Holm O. Bursum

Lawyer by profession, orator by inclination: That was John E. Griffith of Socorro, a friend and staunch supporter of Holm O. Bursum, whom he nominated for governor at the Republican Party's September 28, 1911, convention in Las Vegas. Bursum lost in that first run for the governor's seat, but it was no fault of Griffith's. His fiery speech brought down the house. His legal training and courtroom experience had prepared him well for this role as speaker cum showman. The convention crowd loved his performance. It was as if everything in his life until then had prepared him for that moment.

Born in 1864 in Ohio, Griffith had risen quickly in his chosen profession of the law after a brief stint of teaching school in the Buckeye State. He graduated first from a business college in Cleveland and then took a bachelor's degree from Denison University. He followed that by graduating from the Cincinnati Law School and practicing law in Ohio before coming to New Mexico in 1898. By 1900 he was a clerk in the district court in Socorro. Five years after his caricature appeared in the *Optic Cartoon Book*, he had progressed from that post to district attorney for Socorro and Sierra Counties. With statehood, he was elected district attorney for the 7th Judicial District. He served as president of the Socorro school board from 1905 until 1911 and was a 32nd degree Mason. He held various posts with the local lodge. Such networking led naturally enough to his becoming a Republican Party insider and to his alliance with Bursum.

Griffith was close to Bursum on a political, business, and social plane. It was a natural extension then that he would also serve as Bursum's legal counsel in the firm of Dougherty and Griffith. On some levels, the relationship between the two men seemed to meld seamlessly. Griffith and his wife, along with Mrs. Bursum, had been VIP passengers on a special train to Santa Fe for Governor George Curry's inaugural ball in 1907. These activities made it easy for Bursum to choose him to deliver the candidate's nominating speech.

He had been waiting, and he was ready. "When a member of the Bernalillo County delegation yielded the floor, Griffith seized it with a vengeance." (Hamm 2012) Griffith conceded that Bursum was relatively young (forty-four) but that he had already accomplished much. He further conceded that the Democrats in the upcoming election would try to score political points off Bursum's "lowly birth and self education." That's about all he was willing to concede. Griffith went from zero to sixty, to employ an automotive metaphor, in scant seconds. "I think it is not seriously questioned...that we will win this election," he told his fellow delegates. With Bursum as governor, "the fires of Republicanism will not only not go out...they will be so rekindled and replenished that democracy...shall not be heard of seriously in New Mexico no more forever." It was what the delegates had come to hear.

"Lest too close a comparison be made with the Great Emancipator." (Hamm, 2012) Griffith again allowed that Bursum was no Lincoln. "We do not claim for him perfection," he continued, "but we do assert that...while he will stand like a stone wall or the Rock of Ages for what he believes is right...that he will stand hitched...."

Griffith likened a Progressive to a "crawfish which advances backwards" and denounced Progressives as "always wanting to try some supposed nostrum as a universal panacea for all political ills, while...they close their eyes to the experiences and teachings of history and endeavor to reinstate the practices and policies that...have always proven fatal to the patient. I believe in trying new discoveries, but do not believe in trying arsenic for stomach ache when experience...has shown it to be a deadly poison."

He was suspicious of the press, but conceded that on occasion it could reveal its "intelligent" side (a concession for him a rarity). For the most part, however, he lumped the media with Democrats—some might be friends but it was best to avoid them. As he warmed to his topic he allowed his disdain for the Fourth Estate to show. "Knowing him (Bursum) as we do," he advised the convention, "the twaddle occasionally seen in the so-called press should be to us no more than the sound of suds running into a sink, or the death rattle in the throat of a bath tub." It was just not the press which drew his ire; it was also those who would cast aspersions upon his beloved New Mexico.

Griffith defended his fellow New Mexicans against those who would denigrate them. "...(W)e are not savages or anarchists, but citizens worthy to be classed with the pilgrim fathers and...those who braved the storm and tempest of the sea and the unknown dangers of an unknown land in order that they might plant the standard of the cross in the valley of the Rio Grande." He charged that there were some who did feel this way, but that "charity demands that we should...forget, or at least forget (sic) their actions." He had still another concern to address—that all New Mexicans should be treated equally regardless of from where they hailed.

Native born Spanish Americans, as they were then known, sometimes feared their vote might be taken away from them depending on the ebb and flow of political tides. In an attempt to quell this fear, Griffith insisted that Bursum would not "disenfranchise those whose ancestors happened to be from old Castile and sunny Spain, from the British Isles, Scandinavia or other countries of the northland..." Was this a reference to Bursum's Norwegian ancestry? Perhaps that is why he noted that Bursum, while not New Mexico born, "'came here' about as soon as he could."

Griffith then began ticking off Bursum's attributes, as if the delegates did not already know them. "...you can always know where to find him. He fights fair and in the open. He is not a bush-whacker. You can call him up at any hour of the day or night and at once find out he stands upon any proposition, and why."

It had been nearly a half hour of fiery oratory, just what the delegates had come to hear, and Griffith was about to conclude his remarks. He did so with this. "...(T)hough his pipe has not always been a Merchem (Bursum habitually smoked a corncob pipe), and his Pants not always creased, he has been an honest man, a manly man and stood for what he believed to be the best interests of the whole people, regardless of race, religion or financial standing."

Griffith started strong and he finished strong. He had done both his candidate and himself proud. But in the end, of course, it was not enough. Bursum won the nomination but not the election.

Death came almost two years to the day after his nominating speech. He died September 18, 1913, of liver disease. He was not yet fifty.

PROFESSOR HIRAM HADLEY.
SANTA FE

Hiram Hadley: Pioneer educator, "Friend"

No one has had a larger impact on New Mexico's territorial and early 20th century educational scene than Hiram Hadley—founder of what is now New Mexico State University and first superintendent of public instruction. He accomplished it through dint of hard work and always within the framework in his strong adherence to the tenets of the Society of Friends whose belief system shaped his life and his profession. Furthermore, he did not even come to New Mexico until his middle years.

The *Las Vegas Optic*, in publishing an article and caricature on Hadley March 13, 1906, headed "The Pioneer Educator of New Mexico," offered this: "(he) is one of the pioneer educators in New Mexico (and) had been a prominent and leading figure in her educational affairs." Hadley was all of this and more.

A sixth generation Quaker of English descent, he was born in 1833 on a farm in Chatham County, Ohio, where his Southern-born grandparents had moved because of their opposition to slavery. Following a year of teaching at seventeen, he attended a Friends boarding school in Richmond, Indiana, now Earlham College. There he helped pay his way by cutting cordwood at fifty cents per cord and splitting rails at one dollar per hundred. Later he attended another Quaker institution, Haverford College, in Pennsylvania. His early teaching days were remembered this way: "That he was firm in discipline and demanded high standards goes without saying."

After leaving Haverford and back in Indiana, Hadley taught at Friends schools before going to work for a New York educational publisher as a traveling book salesman. This led to opening a book store in Chicago. An employee there was Robert Underwood Johnson, later ambassador to Italy. Years later Underwood recalled Hadley exhorting the value of hard work. "Robert, I want to tell thee something. There are three kinds of employees." Hadley then enumerated the characteristics of the first two. But the third, he continued, "(is) the one who always does more than he has bargained for or than is expected of him. It is only the last who succeeds." Hadley always lived up to his own dictum.

Hadley relied on those virtues in his everyday life. His first store was destroyed in the great fire of Chicago of 1871. Three years later another fire left him and his co-owner brother penniless. A few years teaching at the college level in Indiana followed by the death of his first wife and a second marriage set the stage for Hadley's move to New Mexico's Mesilla Valley at age fifty-four, where the New Mexico phase of his work was to begin.

He had moved to New Mexico to work in real estate and to be nearer a son in Albuquerque who was seeking restoration of his health. However, Hadley's reputation as an educator soon came to the attention of Las Cruces citizens who wanted an alternative to the local Catholic school. They quickly raised $750 which led to opening of the Las Cruces College in 1888 with Hadley as president. Meanwhile, the Territorial Legislature was moving to establish an agricultural college and experiment station in Las Cruces. This it did in 1899, and a year later the two institutions merged as the New Mexico College of Agricultural and Mechanical Arts with Hadley as president.

Hadley launched into his new duties with his customary energy, but local politics involving Albert B. Fall and others, writes Simon F. Kropp, "undermined his support" and led to his replacement. There followed four years at the University of New Mexico as Vice President before resuming teaching at the agricultural college until 1905. His involvement with the institution had not ended, however, because he served on its board of regents from 1907 until 1913. During that time he formulated guidelines for college presidents and teachers that apply even today. Among them, an ideal president should be:

A man of broad, rich scholarship.

He should be one of those active, energetic men who works and loves to work, one for whom the days seem too short and not enough of them.

He should be a leader, one who goes before...

...he should be a large-hearted, quiet, unassuming man who knows what he wants."

His guidelines for a good teacher were equally clear:

"The teacher should possess good scholarship.

He should be passionately fond of ...teaching.

He should be a worker, not a mere time-server."

He himself still had much to offer New Mexico. Meanwhile, he also served four years on the New Mexico Board of Education and was also president of the New Mexico Education Association. When he was seventy-two, Governor Miguel A. Otero appointed him Superintendent of Public Instruction. He served for only two years, but his contributions were far from over and many of them were guided by his Quaker beliefs.

No Quaker principle is more pronounced than peace. Hadley was at the forefront of the country's National Peace Congress in the lead-up to America's involvement in World War I and attended its meetings until 1915. He also organized and served as president of the New Mexico chapter of the American School Peace League. He had other causes as well and promoted them vigorously. Among them were women's suffrage and prison reform. He twice was New Mexico's representative to the American Prison Congress. He was strongly opposed to tobacco and alcohol use. As if this was not enough, he managed to run a farm and at various times was president of the Las Cruces Chamber of Commerce, the Las Cruces Building and Loan Association, the Mesilla Valley Produce Exchange, and the Mesilla Valley Exchange Club. He also built an apartment building in El Paso.

Six years before his death in a Kansas City hospital on December 3, 1922, a friend wrote, saying, "I have always wondered at your indomitable will and your remarkable vigor of mind and body." Granddaughters Anna R. Hadley and Caroline H. Allen, who authored a seventy-seven page biography entitled *Hiram Hadley: Pioneer Educator*, had the same view. Of him, they said, although he was under average height and build, "he was a bundle of energy."

Hiram Hadley: He lived and worked by his principles.

GOVERNOR H. J. HAGERMAN,
SANTA FE

Herbert J. Hagerman: Governor, diplomat, sacrificial lamb

Herbert J. Hagerman had been a minor American diplomat to the Court of Tsar Nicholas II in St. Petersburg for three years when he returned home to the United States in 1901 and quietly took up ranching and fruit growing at Roswell. Then events began to unfold that promised a sea change for him.

It began in the early 1900s with allegations of wrong doing against New Mexico Governor Miguel A. Otero. Certain that President Theodore Roosevelt would not reappoint him and also to preserve party unity, Otero resigned. "No one expected what followed." The names of several prominent Republicans were submitted to the White House. "Always a political maverick," Roosevelt picked outsider Hagerman. As an attorney by training, a diplomat by experience, and not beholden to Santa Fe, he looked like "the ideal replacement." (Hamm)

As it turned out, he was not. "He was utterly unfamiliar with the methods in vogue" in the rough waters of New Mexico politics, notes Ralph Emerson Twitchell in *Leading Facts of New Mexican History*. The Cornell-trained lawyer was "not qualified by experience" nor did he possess "the talent necessary" to carry out the President's wishes in uncovering alleged fraud in land sales and disposal. One might have thought the intrigues of the Tsar's palace when Hagerman was second secretary would have prepared him for what was to follow, but they did not.

"A man of lofty ideals and sincere in his efforts," said Twitchell, Hagerman lacked the tact and understanding to deal with the turbulent New Mexico political landscape. He soon made all the wrong enemies, including the powerful Chairman of the Republican Central Committee, Holm O. Bursum. Bursum was also superintendent of the territorial penitentiary. Hagerman was seen by many to have done little to support Bursum who was facing his own political difficulties. Hagerman thus alienated himself from the mainstream of the Republican Party in New Mexico that had aligned itself with Bursum.

Bursum biographer Donald Moorman has written there was never any proof that Hagerman was dishonest, only that he was politically naïve and had chosen the wrong friends. The *Las Vegas Optic* seemed to echo that sentiment when it wrote on March 6, 1906, that "There isn't a man in New Mexico that hasn't the fullest confidence, not only in the ability, but also in the integrity and entire honesty" of Hagerman. The newspaper continued that "He is the kind of man to place absolute honesty and justice above every purely political consideration or any question of expediency."

So it was no wonder that Hagerman felt wronged and badly misused when Roosevelt requested his resignation. He had taken office on January 22, 1906, and left it in April of the following year. "Roosevelt's choice of an outsider had clearly backfired." (Hamm) Hagerman felt the need to vindicate himself and self-published a 113-page monograph entitled *A statement in regard to certain matters concerning the governorship and political affairs in New Mexico in 1906–1907.*

He remained bitter at his treatment at the hands of Roosevelt and the Republican establishment. But he stayed on in New Mexico and accepted two more appointments as Chairman of the Special Revenue Commission of New Mexico from 1919-1921 and from 1924 until 1932 as Special Commissioner to Indian tribes in New Mexico, Arizona, Utah, and Colorado. He died in Santa Fe on January 28, 1935, seventy-three years after his birth in Milwaukee.

HON. W. S. HOPEWELL,
ALBUQUERQUE

Willard S. Hopewell: He found greater opportunities in promoting New Mexico

"Promoter." That simple but all-encompassing description was inked on Willard S. Hopewell's death certificate when he died at his Albuquerque home in 1919. Born in Chester, England, Hopewell as a boy had envisioned greater opportunities across the Atlantic. At age fifteen, the *Las Vegas Optic* relates, he immigrated to Canada. Still searching, two years after the Civil War he moved again—this time to the United States. And find those opportunities he did.

Hopewell's faith in his new homeland was to be justified a hundredfold over. The newcomer did find great opportunities in America and in New Mexico Territory. He found them in beating the drum for his adopted country and territory. The *Albuquerque Morning Journal* recognized his calling and his success at it. Hopewell was never seen as promoting himself for self-aggrandizement; he promoted causes beyond himself. The *Journal* recognized this quality when it called him a "booster leader."

One example was his 1911 election to a leadership post with the National Irrigation Congress, a "powerful pressure group" for Western water issues, according to Wikipedia. Water has always been critical to New Mexico, so Hopewell's service was essential. The *Journal* heralded his inclusion to the Board of Governors, commenting that membership had put him in an "influential place" for the territory.

Some illustrious names had always been on the group's rolls; its sessions had attracted such prominent speakers as William Jennings Bryan and Gifford Pinchot, President Theodore Roosevelt's forest service director. Hopewell was not the only New Mexican honored to serve. Ralph Emerson Twitchell had been instrumental in bringing the Congress to Albuquerque in 1908.

In New Mexico Hopewell found his calling—working to advance agriculture. He served on the Cattle Sanitary Board, thus promoting and safeguarding one of the territory's most valuable resources. From his base in Hillsboro when he lived there he organized and managed the Las Animas Cattle Company. Under his leadership, the company invested $1 million in land and cattle in Sierra County, a most sizeable sum. The *Las Vegas Optic* offered the following about what a cattle owner would do to protect his herd.

In the early days in neighboring Socorro County, the *Optic* reported, Hopewell was "reckoned as the terror of cattle rustlers and law breakers of every description." As leader of the rangers he was "most instrumental in winning the land for law and order." But it was not just water and ranching that attracted Hopewell's drive to promote New Mexico and to pursue his boyhood dreams. He engaged in all the typical pursuits of late 19th century American entrepreneurs. Cattle, mining, and railroading: He followed them all and all with success.

Hopewell developed and operated the Home Stake mines as well as the Caledonia and the Hibernian. With the latter two he struck it rich; they yielded rich deposits of gold. He helped build the Santa Fe Central Railroad, serving as vice president and general manager. Not content with commercial pursuits, Hopewell, always a Democrat, served in the Territorial Legislature. There he helped promote—naturally—statehood.

Finally with active hands-on involvement behind him and when he had moved to Albuquerque, residents there recognized his role in "upbuilding" that city by electing him president of the Albuquerque Commercial Club. Upon his death and as a mark of the esteem with which he was held by his beloved New Mexico, his body lay in state at the family home on Copper Street. Hundreds paid their respects. The crowd, reported the *Journal*, "filled the house and overflowed into the lawn." Hopewell was seventy-two. He had achieved all he had set out to do.

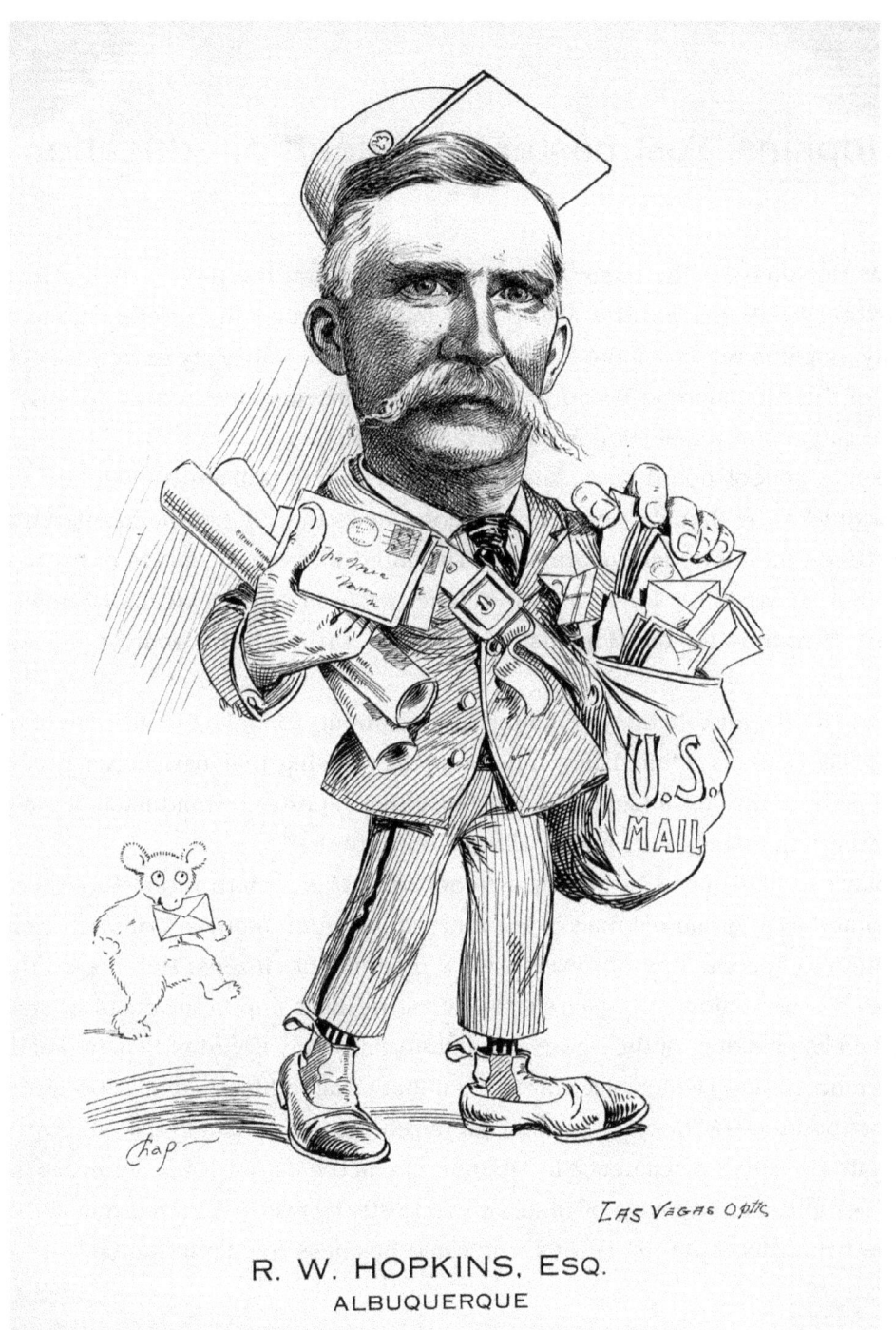

R. W. HOPKINS, ESQ.
ALBUQUERQUE

R.W. Hopkins: Postmaster and friend of education

R.W. Hopkins was the postmaster in Albuquerque at the time of his inclusion in the *Optic Cartoon Book* in 1906. He also played important roles in the educational life of his community. Hopkins served on the Board of Regents of the University of New Mexico and was president of the Albuquerque Board of Education. Consequently, he did not take kindly to what he considered as a defection from the ranks by his staff.

In 1908, school board clerk and aspiring newsman William A. Keleher approached Hopkins with what he thought would be the good news that he had been offered a position as a reporter on the *Albuquerque Journal*. "Delighted with the prospects of my new job and confident that he would rejoice with me," Keleher wrote in *New Mexicans I Knew: Memoirs, 1892-1969*, "I hurried (to tell Hopkins) of my good fortune." The board president did not rejoice.

Instead he sternly told the young man he was about "to make the mistake of a lifetime." Keleher recalls Hopkins admonishing him with the warning that newspaper reporters were "heavy drinkers as a rule," adding that "if I became a reporter I would likely wake up to find myself dead drunk rolling in the gutter within a few months."

Hopkins turned out to be wrong. Keleher did not sink into moral turpitude. Keleher, later acclaimed as a "grand old man of law and letters" (*Albuquerque Tribune*), went on after newspapering to become one of New Mexico's preeminent citizens. He entered the law and helped found a prestigious Albuquerque law firm. He held important posts in state government, served as president of the New Mexico State University Board of Regents, and achieved renown as a noted New Mexico historian. But all that awaited him, and in 1908, Keleher was a lowly school board clerk. Hopkins strongly preferred that he remain in that station.

Despite Hopkins's prominence in Albuquerque in the early 1900s, not much is known of him before or after that. A native of Ohio, by the 1880s he was in Albuquerque working for his father-in-law, H.L. Moore, in the latter's wholesale business trading in lumber, ore, and flour.

He was appointed postmaster July 18, 1901, and remained in that position until March 11, 1911. He then moved to El Paso.

The *El Paso Herald* reported that Robert Wilmot Hopkins, seventy-two, died November 16, 1920. The story noted that Hopkins had managed the Primm cigar stores of El Paso for several years. The *Albuquerque Journal* reported the following day that "R.W. Hopkins, for many years postmaster of Albuquerque, at one time president of the school board, and a resident of this city for 35 years, died yesterday at El Paso after an illness of two weeks."

W. P. JOHNSTON, ESQ.,
ALBUQUERQUE

William P. Johnson: Lumber company executive

A native of Zenia, Ohio, William P. Johnson was president the American Lumber Company of Albuquerque when his caricature appeared in the *Optic Cartoon Book*. He died in St. Joseph's Hospital, Albuquerque, September 25, 1909, while under the care of Dr. C.H. Conner.

The direct cause of death was asthenia and the indirect cause was chronic interstitial nephritis. He was buried in Cleveland, Ohio. His name was spelled Johnston in the *Optic Cartoon Book* but with no "t" on his death certificate.

FLEMMING JONES, ESQ.
LAS CRUCES

W.A. Fleming Jones: Authority in land and conservation

Born in Birmingham, England in 1871, W. A. Fleming Jones came to the United States by way of Canada (1891) where he developed and operated mining properties. In his native England he had pursued a literary curriculum before taking up the study of law. This was to prove a valuable resource in future pursuits. By1898 he was in New Mexico where he lived first in Lincoln and then in Socorro before moving finally to Las Cruces. There he directed his various businesses and would remain the rest of his life.

Representative New Mexicans called him an "extensive operator in lands throughout the west and (a) recognized authority on public land matters." He was nationally recognized for that expertise and maintained an office in Washington to facilitate his work on those issues at the federal level. Ralph Emerson Twitchell notes that once in the Southwest Jones' career path had him dealing exclusively in lands. He adds that Jones was a public lands commissioner who did "much in shaping public thought and actions" on those issues.

Also active in conservation, Jones was secretary-treasurer of the New Mexico Conservation Commission and served on the executive committee of the National Conservation Commission. Twitchell called him "a close and discriminating student" of conservation and natural resources.

Jones headed the Alameda Realty & Investment Company and was a director of the Bowman Bank and Trust, both in Las Cruces. His business interests led him into Republican politics and public service. He was a member of the Territorial Republican Central Committee, a U.S. Commissioner for the Third Judicial District, and for four years a regent for the School of Mines in Socorro. Jones also served in the New Mexico National Guard.

Jones died November 28, 1917. He had found his home and his work in New Mexico.

MAJOR W. H. LLEWELLYN,
LAS CRUCES

W.H.H. Llewellyn: Roosevelt confidante, Rough Rider, politician

After San Juan Hill, Theodore Roosevelt retained a lifelong affection for his comrades-in-arms among his beloved Rough Riders, but among his special friends and confidantes was colonel William H.H. Llewellyn of Las Cruces. The Spanish American War Centennial Website notes that Llewellyn was "close enough to the President to dine with him at the White House, to escort Mrs. Roosevelt to the theatre (when the President was otherwise occupied), and who is one of the few" Rough Riders mentioned in Roosevelt's autobiography. The website and *Leading Facts of New Mexican History* provide the basis for this profile.

Some of Roosevelt's esteem for Llewellyn stemmed from a key role the latter played in alerting his headquarters to the movement of Spanish troops which precipitated the Rough Riders' successful charge up San Juan Hill. Llewellyn's action earned him a promotion to Major. The President was "strongly attached" to Llewellyn, a man over six feet tall and two-hundred pounds and very likable. He wrote that Llewellyn was "a large, jovial, frontier Micawber type of person, with a varied past, which includes considerable man-killing." Once when Llewellyn was ill, Roosevelt wrote the Major's wife asking her to convey his warmest regards, adding that "You know how I value him as a soldier and how I prize his friendship." All this led the *Silver City Independent* to observe that "Our own Major Llewellyn is 'some pumpkins' back in Washington just now."

Llewellyn's seventy-five year lifespan is divided into four separate areas, none neatly compartmentalized or seamless. One was his service with the Rough Riders. Although relatively brief, it earned him short-term celebrity status. He returned to Las Cruces from Cuba as "something of a war hero." (New Mexico Centennial Website) Although that engagement earned him no decorations, it did cause him to contract yellow fever, resulting in hospitalization in New York City to recuperate. Llewellyn had been a member of the Territorial Militia before going to Cuba. He earned a colonelcy when he was appointed New Mexico Judge

Advocate General, serving under both Governor Miguel A. Otero and Governor Herbert J. Hagerman. Llewellyn's eighteen-year-old son Morgan also joined with his father at the onset of the war. But a coin toss kept the youth's Troop H at home while the elder Llewellyn shipped out of Tampa.

Politics was another arena of involvement. Some contacts, like his friendship with Roosevelt, grew out from his military service. Llewellyn's association with Senator Holm O. Bursum stemmed, however, from New Mexico's push for statehood. Like so many around the territory, Llewellyn was a firm adherent and worked assiduously to achieve it. He often pushed the agenda in his meetings with Roosevelt. The President was a believer. He wanted to be the "statehood president." He liked both the territory and the men it produced. "New Mexico was his kind of place. He wanted to deliver but couldn't." (Hamm 2012)

Llewellyn strove to remain in favor with Bursum because he wanted the Senator's assistance in regaining the speakership of the Territorial Legislature. Thus he promoted statehood whenever he was in Washington. On one occasion, for example, he wrote Bursum from the capital saying that "It appears from the present outlook that the statehood bill will pass." Llewellyn took pains to temper his confidence by adding that "although there are a number of amendments yet to be tacked on and as nothing is sure except death and taxes the bill may yet fail." It did. The quest was to continue for several more years. It was President William H. Taft who signed the statehood bill, not Roosevelt.

Llewellyn had left his native Wisconsin at fifteen to prospect for gold in Montana. He labored there eight years without becoming rich and then moved east to Omaha to work as a land speculator and bill collector, again with no success. In 1877 President Rutherford B. Hayes appointed him Special Agent with the Justice Department. He was sent to the Pine Ridge Reservation in South Dakota to protect the Sioux's pony herds from predation by white raiders.

There Llewellyn acquitted himself well and proved to be "a courageous law officer," says the Centennial Website. That earned him reassignment to New Mexico, where he was to remain the rest of his life. With the Mescalero tribe near present-day Ruidoso he quickly enacted a number of measures to improve the Indians' lives and earn their trust—establishing an Indian police force, adding a doctor to the agency, establishing a boarding school, and helping the tribe affiliate with the cattle growers association. For his efforts, the Mescalero affectionately called him "Taa" (father) Crooked Nose.

Llewellyn was a lifelong Republican. He served as a delegate to the Republican National Conventions in 1884, 1896, 1900, 1904, and 1908. When President Grover Cleveland swept the Democrats into power in 1885 Llewellyn left the Mescalero reservation and moved to Las Cruces to enter private law practice. He had prepared for this by three years study in Omaha and four more in Las Cruces. He was admitted to the New Mexico bar in 1886 and in 1893 to practice before the United States Supreme Court. Llewellyn had a number of important and interesting assignments as a director and attorney for several mining companies and as an attorney for Western Union. In 1896 he also assisted the prosecution in the notorious and still unsolved Albert Jennings Fountain murder case.

That year also marked Llewellyn's entry into politics with his election as Speaker of the Territorial House of Representatives. In 1912 he became a member of the first State Legislature. He later served as a New Mexico District Attorney and as a United States District Attorney, prosecuting a number of important cases, including violation of the country's neutrality laws involving the smuggling of Chinese into the United States. Llewellyn devoted thirty years to the law. Of this, Ralph Emerson Twitchell said in *Leading Facts of New Mexican History* that Llewellyn was noted for his "integrity and honor" and "his fidelity to duty."

William Henry Harrison Llewellyn died June 11, 1927, in the U.S. Army William Beaumont Hospital in El Paso. He left behind his widow Ida May and seven children. He is buried in the Masonic Cemetery in Las Cruces.

Of him, Twitchell also wrote: "His entire career has been guided by high and honorable principles, as manifest in his close conformity to the highest standards...(and) in his public-spirited citizenship shown by his subordination of personal aggrandizement to the public good, in his loyalty in friendship and his support of all those forces which work for the betterment and uplift of the individual."

HON. SOLOMON LUNA,
ALBUQUERQUE

Solomon Luna: Sheep man, Republican power

"Sol" to his friends. "Don Solomon" to those who held him in awe or respect. "King Solomon" to his detractors. One thing which is clear about Solomon Luna was his power and wealth; not so certain are the circumstances of his death. That he drowned in a vat of "Cooper's Fluid" sheep dip sometime during the night hours of August 29, 1912, is clear enough. How it came about is not. Perhaps also it is fitting that his demise would be at the hands of something he himself had instituted for the protection of his vast herds of sheep.

It was a tragic, untimely end for a man who seemingly had everything. Luna's death was tinged with mystery. Explanations of the cause circulated for weeks until a court finally ruled it was an accidental drowning resulting from a fall. At the time of his death, Luna grazed 80,000 sheep yielding 400,000 pounds of wool each year. He was also heavily invested in banking, real estate, and insurance. An estimate of his net worth when he died was nearly $1 million. His influence in the Republican Party was not as easily measured, but it was very, very strong.

Why and how did this symbol of wealth and influence meet such an inglorious end only two months shy of his fifty-fourth birthday? New Mexico historian Richard Melzer provides the details in his richly drawn article "King Solomon's Mysterious Demise" written for the Office of the State Historian.

A supreme irony of Luna's death is that it was he himself who lobbied in the late 1890s for establishment of the New Mexico Sheep Sanitary Board to deal with the scab tick menace then ravaging New Mexico's herds. The solution was to dip them. He was elected the board's first president. Another irony is that the vat was constructed with sloping concrete walls coming together at the bottom to form a V. The design was intended to prevent sheep from scrambling out during the dipping process. It could also keep a five-foot, nine-inch man (Luna's height) from escaping as well. Unfortunately, it prevented Luna, maybe half asleep or perhaps rendered unconscious from a hard knock to the head from a nocturnal visit to the outhouse, from saving himself.

Sheep dipping is always a big event for any ranch and the owner is always present. That fateful August the dipping took place at the Horse Springs Ranch of English owner Montague Stevens on the San Augustin Plains west of Magdalena. The process had gone uneventfully and things had proceeded well except that Luna had complained of a persistent stomach upset, perhaps from eating too much green chile. It had caused him to make more trips outside to relieve himself that he might have done.

When the some fifty hands and the Animal Husbandry Bureau agent gathered at dawn the next morning to resume work they spotted a body floating in the dip. A hasty examination revealed the awful news—it was Luna. Various explanations of his death soon surfaced and myriad scenarios were posited. One, and the most plausible, was that it was just a tragic accidental drowning. "(I)t was not long...that at least three more sinister theories surfaced to explain how he (Luna) might have died..." writes Melzer. One was that he was murdered. Another was that he committed suicide by drowning. Another, perhaps the most bizarre of all, was that Luna was a crypto-Jew and that he had fabricated an elaborate ruse to escape to Europe to practice his long submerged Jewish faith.

What is no mystery is the story of Luna's life and his accumulation of power, wealth, and influence. Solomon, the third of three sons and older brother to sister Eloisa, was born October 18, 1858, in what is now Los Lunas, into a family whose roots went deep into New Mexico history. He did nothing to diminish its luster, only to build on it. In the seventeenth century Don Domingo de Luna, a first cousin of the Duke of Albuquerque, came to New Mexico. For services to the Spanish crown, he was a ceded a huge grant of land between the Rio Puerco and the Rio Grande, one of the best irrigated areas in the southwest. It was to be the basis of the family wealth, chiefly sheep.

Young Solomon had a mostly uneventful childhood, playing and attending class under a private tutor in the family home. One tragedy occurred when he was about twelve when a group of marauding Indians raided the area and killed his uncle and several other men who were working a nearby field. But boyhood pursuits were put aside when he was trundled off to St. Louis, Missouri, like so many others of his social class, to attend the Christian Brothers

School and the St. Louis University preparatory school in 1872. It appears that Luna withdrew over the Christmas holidays of 1874 and returned to New Mexico.

Back home Solomon soon immersed himself working side by side with his father, Antonio José, where he soon became adept both in the sheep industry and in politics. In the field, he did what was necessary; nothing was beneath him. If a sheep needed shearing or dipping, he lent a hand. But it was not all work. Young Luna especially enjoyed the *baile* (the dance) and it was on one such occasion that he met Adelaida Otero of Peralta, who would become his wife on January 15, 1882, thus joining two prominent families. But there were to be no children of the union.

Three years after Solomon's marriage, his father died. Since his two brothers were engaged in politics, it was up to Luna to carry on the family ranching enterprise. Frequent run-ins with cattle ranchers were inevitable, and Luna went to court as necessary to resolve them. But disease was an equally big problem. This prompted creation of the New Mexico Sheep Sanitary Board and later the New Mexico Wool Growers Association to both protect the industry and to market its products.

With his family's livelihood assured, it was time for Luna to assert himself into the realm of politics. It is probably not an overstatement to assert that Luna could have had any political post he wanted in New Mexico. At the beginning of his political career he did fill a number of important local posts, including probate clerk (1885); sheriff (1892) in which he earned a reputation as a "fearless, tactful peace officer;" county treasurer (1894); and election to the National Republican Committee from New Mexico in 1896. But he turned down more opportunities than he accepted. In 1900, the Findagrave web site tells us, he was offered the Republican nomination to Congress but declined. Likewise, he was offered the candidacy for the first state governor of New Mexico but said no to that post as well.

What he did accept was an invitation to the Constitutional Convention of 1910 where he assumed the chairmanship of the powerful Committee of Committees. The *Albuquerque Journal*, as reported by the State Historian, said Luna ranked the honor as one of "the proudest of his life." Charles A. Spiess presided, but Luna was "clearly the most powerful member" present, writes Richard Melzer and others in *A History of New Mexico Since Statehood*. Luna, they point out, was "a dominant figure in the Republican Party on the local, territorial, and even the national levels." It is perhaps apocryphal that some politicians could influence proceedings from the back of a room merely by a nod of the head or the cocking an eyebrow, but "so powerful was Mr. Luna's influence that no Republican candidate could hope to succeed" without his support.

Why did Luna want to be part of the convention and to chair the Committee on Committees? His purpose was to ensure Hispanic rights—particularly voting rights (Article 7, section 3) which protected the right of every New Mexican to vote regardless of "religion, race, language, or color;" and Article 12, section 10, which stated that "children of Spanish descent" would never be denied admission to public schools nor ever be "classified in separate schools, but shall forever enjoy perfect equality with other children in all public schools."

Luna, like most members of his party, favored admission to the Union even though he had been charged with "knifing statehood" because he preferred to "vote the sheep," an accusation against sheep men. Probably the best argument against this allegation is that Los Lunas did not cast one vote toward defeat of the constitution and that Valencia County voted 1,465 for and 229 against its ratification. Such totals could not have been possible without Luna's approval. He was always considered "the one who remained clean amid corruption, one whose tact and character were such as to disarm fights from all bitterness."

Perhaps Luna's loss to his party was best summed up by this headline: "Balance Wheel Gone"

Note: The principal sources for this profile are from the New Mexico Office of the State Historian: Chapter I, *Solomon's Ancestry*; Chapter II, *Solomon's Education*; Chapter III, *Solomon Becomes a Man of the World*; Chapter IV, *Solomon and the Sheep Industry*; Chapter V, *Political Career*; Chapter VI, *Statehood of New Mexico*; and "King Solomon's Mysterious Demise" by Richard Melzer. If there is no other attribution, the material comes from them.

HON. O. M. MARRON,
ALBUQUERQUE

Owen N. Marron: He came to serve; in service he found his vocation

The *New Mexico Historical Review* and Don Bullis' excellent profile in *New Mexico Historical Biographies* offer intriguing insights into the life of Owen N. Marron. Both provide the picture of a trained educator who came to the New Mexico Territory in 1889 with one goal in mind: to serve its Native American youth. That he did. But he remained to enter another profession. What followed makes for an even more compelling story.

Marron, a native of Port Henry, New York, and trained for a career in teaching, arrived in Albuquerque in 1889 to take up his new post as assistant superintendent of the U.S. Indian School. A year later he was transferred to the Indian School in Santa Fe. Bullis tells us what happened next. There Marron's life changed; he found the law. He moonlighted. His day job remained with the Indian School, but he also read law on the side with prominent Santa Fe attorney William Burr Childers. Marron was a fast study; he was admitted to the bar in 1891.

Entry into the law opened the door for Marron to return to Albuquerque. There he became law partners with Needham C. Collier. When a man is prepared and is ready, opportunity finds him. That is what happened with Marron. When President Grover Cleveland named Collier to the Second Judicial Court in 1991, Collier named his old law partner as his court clerk. Marron had been an attorney for all of two years. He remained with the court for several years.

In 1908 Marron returned to private practice and entered partnership with Francis E. Wood. That association continued until the end of Marron's life. Law, as it is for many in that profession, served as a springboard into politics. For Marron, that meant Democratic politics. He was three times elected mayor of Albuquerque—in 1889, 1900, and 1901. As New Mexico's first state gubernatorial election dawned, Marron was mentioned as a favorite for the post. He passed and backed William C. McDonald, who defeated Holm O. Bursum. When New Mexico became a state—Marron was always a staunch supporter of statehood—he was elected state treasurer.

After leaving politics Marron took up business pursuits and was an organizer of the State

National Bank of Albuquerque, which he served as president. He had a number of financial interests in several Albuquerque businesses. He was also president and board member of the Albuquerque Commercial Club.

Marron was a member of the Catholic Church and was a charter member of the Albuquerque Council No. 641 of the Knights of Columbus. He was the council's first grand knight as well as the order's first territorial and first state deputy in New Mexico.

Marron died New Year's Day 1945. He was eighty-three. His wife, the former Frances Halloran, whom he had married in 1901, predeceased him by six years.

HON. WM. E. MARTIN,
SOCORRO

William E. Martin: Orator, scholar

"To be Anglo-Saxon...and (to be) born in New Mexico is not a common combination of circumstances" began a May 25, 1906 article on William E. Martin in the *Las Vegas Optic* a few weeks before his likeness appeared in the *Optic Cartoon Book*. Readers were privileged to get a glimpse of Martin at age forty. What a revealing glimpse it was of a prominent New Mexican whose family, marriage, and career linked him to several important figures in American history. His life began bright with promise. The newspaper hinted as much when it said that "The future promises guerdon (rewards) to this gifted and capable young man."

Martin's father fought with General Winfield Scott in the Mexican-American War and was with the famous military hero in the storming of Chapultepec in Mexico City in September of 1847. Martin's wife was a cousin of President James A. Garfield, and Martin himself was involved in a barroom altercation with the legendary Elfego Baca who had stood off several Texas cowboys in the famous shootout at Frisco.

Those factors alone would have been enough to mark Martin for distinction in turn-of-the-century New Mexico. But he enjoyed something else—a fluency in Spanish which was good enough to earn him a post as interpreter in the courts of his home town of Socorro. Bilingualism was a valuable gift since the town's citizenry often traded in two languages, both in the courts and in everyday life. Martin's gift for languages led the *Optic* to comment on his fluency "(as) an orator, both in Spanish and English. No interpreter who ever served in the courts or the public...has ever outpeered (sic) William Martin."

Although the *Optic* trumpeted Martin's bilingualism, it included other noteworthy facts about him and his family as well. Martin's father sailed around Cape Horn at the conclusion of hostilities in Mexico. At the outbreak of the Civil War he was appointed a colonel in the 1st California Infantry and marched eastward to Las Cruces. There he later chose to remain and marry. He and his wife moved to Fort Selden, where their son was born. Afterwards the family home was at Aleman Ranch (Martin's Well) on the infamous Jornado del Muerto. There, according to the *Optic*, Colonel Martin found water, the first developed in that vast parched expanse. But schooling beckoned for the boy.

At the proper age, the younger Martin was bundled off to St. Michael's College in Santa Fe to study the classics. He later used his education and language abilities to gain a seat in the territorial legislature and to serve several times as chief clerk during various sessions. He was also deputy and chief clerk at the land office in Las Cruces and clerk of the Fifth and Third Judicial Districts. Among his many appointive posts was coal oil inspector for the territory. The *Optic* further noted that Martin, like so many others in territorial politics, was a Republican and "a man ever loyal in every fibre (sic) to his party."

Although the *Optic* cited these and other milestones in Martin's life, such as a stint as chief clerk and then assistant superintendent of the territorial penitentiary under fellow Socorran and Republican Holm O. Bursum, it markedly did not mention the alleged barroom encounter with Baca. Below is how Stan Sager recounts it in *¡Viva Elfego! The Case for Elfego Baca, Hispanic Hero* (2008). The alleged incident began after work with a couple of drinks one night in Blavaschi's Saloon.

The two had been drinking companionably when, according to Sager's account of the incident, Baca began verbally abusing Martin. Martin, perhaps understanding that Baca was feeling cooped up at a desk job as county clerk after law enforcement jobs, took it for a while. But enough was enough and Martin threw a punch. At this point, according to Sager, Baca pulled a pistol and fired three rounds. Luckily, the combination of too much whiskey and the fortuitous intervention of a fellow patron caused Baca's shots to go wild. Nonetheless, both combatants were arrested. Baca's case went to a grand jury, and he was indicted for assault with a deadly weapon with intent to kill. Eventually his case was resolved with no jail time. Baca was running for mayor of Socorro at the time of the fracas. Perhaps the incident heightened his notoriety around town because he was elected and served a term. He did not run a second time, and, ironically Martin succeeded him. Martin's run-in with Baca was not the only one he was reported to have had, one allegedly with far more serious consequences than merely a thrown punch.

This time the story gains even more credibility because it is related by Governor Miguel A. Otero. As with many other anecdotes about Martin, Otero begins by praising the man's linguistic skills. Calling 'Billie' Martin "a warm personal friend," the governor cites him as a perfect exemplar of the interpretive profession. "He was, without exception, the best interpreter in the territory...his speeches, in both English and Spanish were perfect gems." But Martin had a darker side. Here is Otero in *My Life on the Frontier: 1882-1897*: "Unfortunately, he (Martin) had one serious fault: if he took one drink of strong liquor he had to have more, and when under the influence of too much liquor, he was rather dangerous." The governor was given to understatement.

According to Otero, Martin, on one such occasion, became involved with "a very dangerous citizen" of a small New Mexico village. "Both men went for their pistols, but Martin was a little quicker and fired one shot" killing the other where he stood. Martin fled to Mexico. After a time he returned north and won a pardon. Such episodes must have haunted him. Despite a splendid education, strong political loyalties, and exceptional language abilities, Martin was haunted by dark moments.

On a bright spring day on May 9, 1913, this "Republican leader...member of former legislatures, clerk of the district court...eloquent orator and a Spanish scholar" flung himself from a third story window of the First National Bank Building in Santa Fe and was "picked up dead." (*Deming Headlight*)

JAMES G. M^cNARY, ESQ.,
LAS VEGAS

James G. McNary: The man behind the book, publishing, banking, lumbering

When Jim McNary took a year off from college to tour as a singing evangelist (as might be expected of a preacher's kid with a musical bent), then afterwards earned a BA degree and studied German and French in Europe for fifteen months, little did he envision a life that included college teaching, tenure as a newspaper publisher in a wide-open western town, publishing the *Optic Cartoon Book*, and success in banking and lumber. He even found time for a fistfight with a fellow editor in his adopted home town of Las Vegas, New Mexico.

James Graham McNary was a New Year's Day baby born in 1877 in the college town of Bloomington, Indiana. Parents Elizabeth Graham McNary and the Reverend William P. McNary oversaw a large family where religion, music, and scholarship blended seamlessly. The elder McNary had left theological seminary at the outset of the Civil War and served at Malvern Hill, Antietam, and Fredericksburg. He came out without a scratch and with the rank of colonel after enlisting as a private. His parents hoped young McNary might enter the ministry. He had other ideas. They ultimately involved a move west.

With his background in languages, it was natural for McNary to consider teaching. When the Las Vegas Normal School (now New Mexico Highlands University) opened in 1898 he was a member of its first faculty in languages and music. He also directed a quartet in the Presbyterian Church. There he met and married the church organist, Ruth Raynolds, daughter of Las Vegas banker Joshua Raynolds. He was to play a major role in McNary's life.

After five years teaching and with a year for further study in Germany, McNary followed an inclination towards business and acquired the *Las Vegas Optic*. Five years with the newspaper were mostly uneventful except for two occurrences.

McNary was always open to additional sources of revenue to support his growing family. So when Eastern itinerant newspaper cartoonist Harry S. Palmer proposed a booklet of caricatures of prominent New Mexicans McNary used his business and Republican connections to enlist fifty of them at $100 a head and publish the book known as *The Optic Cartoon Book*. While the extra income was welcome, notoriety and a grand jury appearance were not.

Rivalry between the Old Town and New Town areas of Las Vegas had raged for decades. Residents of Old Town brought in an outsider to start a weekly paper. He soon began disparaging everyone in town, including McNary. The former singing evangelist confronted the man on the street and administered him a sound thrashing. The injuries were so bad to the other man that McNary was arrested and indicted for murder. After a period of uncertainty the charges were dismissed. But when McNary's father-in-law invited him to enter banking in El Paso, where he had bought the First National Bank, McNary accepted. However, New Mexico ties were hard to break.

Even while working in El Paso, the McNarys built a home in Cloudcroft so he could spend summers there and commute to work other times to El Paso. He was elected president of the bank ten years later. Meanwhile, he had entered the timber industry in Louisiana. By the time the Depression hit, McNary had moved to Arizona to continue in timber.

The next few years saw other major events for McNary. He was asked to spend four months with the YMCA seeing to the welfare of American Doughboys in World War I in France and then was appointed by President Warren Harding as Comptroller of the Currency. Returning from Washington, he spent twenty-five more years in the timber industry in Arizona with a town named for him there and was twice elected president of the National Lumber Manufacturers Association. McNary wrote of his life in *This is My Life*. He died in Santa Barbara, California, June 10, 1961, at age eighty-five.

CHIEF JUSTICE WM. J. MILLS,
LAS VEGAS

William J. Mills: Governor, jurist

The *New Mexico Optic* series featured New Mexicans whose stars shone more brightly in their backyards and those who were obviously better known throughout the territory and the West. William J. Mills was one of the latter. For whatever reason Mills did not even merit a mention in the *Las Vegas Optic* front page series, only in the *Optic Cartoon Book* itself. Perhaps he did not grant an interview or submit a resume to McNary to serve as the basis for a write-up. A lack of coverage was a bit strange perhaps but not totally inexplicable. After all, Mills' prominence was yet to come.

Mills was a Southerner by birth (Yazoo City, Mississippi, 1849) who became a Connecticut Yankee when his mother moved the family north after the death of his father. Early schooling was at the Norwich Free Academy. That was followed by law school at Yale University and a degree in 1877. He joined the Democratic Party and soon set up his own legal practice before winning election to the Connecticut Legislature, serving in both chambers. Thus he was one of that relatively rare breed of early New Mexicans whose success was grounded on a solid education and work experience in his profession and not just hard work and native intelligence as was the case with many. But the east might have been too stifling for Mills. In 1885 he married Alice Waddingham of West Haven, Connecticut, whose father was a big land owner in New Mexico. Opportunity in a new land beckoned.

By August of 1886 he was partnering in the law offices of Thomas B. Catron, one of the most influential men in New Mexico and a leading figure in the Republican Party. That relationship lasted two years. In 1894 Mills and his family returned to New Haven where he practiced law for another four years. Relative obscurity quickly faded when President William McKinley nominated him to become Chief Justice of the New Mexico Supreme Court to take his seat in January of 1898.

It was an opportunity to return to Santa Fe, and it marked the beginning of his upward ascendancy. Mills' new judicial post, however, was accompanied by a change in party affiliation.

In Connecticut he had been a Gold Democrat, a short-lived conservative branch of the party, but in New Mexico he made his conservatism official and became a Republican. Mills found favor with President Theodore Roosevelt, who appointed him to two additional terms.

The high court was the positioning point for something more. President William H. Taft had seen something in the chief justice's rulings and conservative leanings that he found attractive. When George Curry resigned as governor of the territory, Taft selected Mills to replace him. He was sworn in on March 1, 1910. His active political life was to last only two more years.

Upon becoming governor, Mills joined with many others, some of them featured in the *Optic Cartoon Book*, in the push for statehood. The 1910 Constitutional Convention set the stage for that grand event. As required to do so, Mills called for election of new office holders in November of 1911.

New Mexico was admitted to the union on January 6, 1912, and Mills left office eleven days later when William B. McDonald became the state's first governor. Mills ran unsuccessfully for the United States Senate later that year. His active political life was over; his public service was at an end.

He remained in New Mexico and died in East Las Vegas, Christmas Eve, 1915.

E. G. MURPHEY, ESQ.,
LAS VEGAS

E. G. Murphey: Pioneer pharmacist

E.G. (Edward) Murphey was a pioneer pharmacist in East Las Vegas who operated a drug store at the corner of Sixth and Douglas Streets. He believed in the power of marketing. That is evidenced by his inclusion the *Optic Cartoon Book* and by the fact that he issued tokens valued at five cents good in exchange for a cigar or a soft drink at his drug store's soda fountain.

Murphey was active in the affairs of his profession throughout the territory and served on the Board of Pharmacy in the early 1900s. He lived in Las Vegas for forty years and was known for his genial disposition and his support of his adopted city. For ten years he was a member of the board of trustees of the Las Vegas Land Grant. He was first exalted ruler of the Elks lodge, was a member of the Knights of Pythias, and was a member of the Episcopal Church.

He was born August 16, 1857, in Union County, Pennsylvania, and died suddenly May 30, 1920, in Las Vegas following an operation.

He was interred in the Masonic Cemetery in Las Vegas but was later reburied beside his wife in Los Angeles following her death there.

HON. W. H. NEWCOMB,
SILVER CITY

William H. Newcomb: A man of strong convictions

William H. Newcomb shared many of the characteristics of those in the *Optic Cartoon Book*. He was a migrant to New Mexico. He was a Republican. He was active in Masonry. He helped build the territory, and his adopted home town of Silver City, New Mexico, could not have grown without him. *History of New Mexico* in 1881 foresaw Newcomb's lasting impact. "He is a man of strong convictions, and being energetic and popular he will no doubt attain that success awarded to ambitious and worthy men."

The *Las Vegas Optic*, in writing of him on June 2, 1906, echoed those sentiments: "Judge Newcomb (he was elected Justice of the Peace in 1889) is one of the best known men in New Mexico and his popularity and the esteem in which he is held at home and abroad bears testimony to his high character, his broad intelligence and his genial spirit." Despite losing his father at age twelve and being forced to come west to restore his failing health, he was that man. He did achieve success.

When he died June 18, 1917, Newcomb had lived the life foreseen for him. But it had unfolded in strange new surroundings. Boston, the place of his birth, contrasted vividly with the Silver City he found when he arrived in 1876. It was still an outpost and still subject to Apache depredations. Silver City must have been quite a shock.

The *Silver City Enterprise* noted that "At the age of thirty he found the routine position he held in the office of the Merchants Exchange in an eastern seacoast city irksome and he set out for the wildest part of the wooly west." In Silver City he found what he was looking for.

When he died, the *Enterprise* observed that he had been a rancher, mine owner, and railroad promoter. He also operated a limestone quarry in 1906-1907, and some Silver City buildings are constructed of that material. In the process, Newcomb "made and lost several fortunes." He acquired some of the most valuable mining properties in southwestern New Mexico and served as president of the Silver City, Pinos Altos and Mogollon Railroad Company. That undertaking envisioned a railroad to carry silver ore from the rich mines of Mogollon to the smelters, thus making the enterprise financially worthwhile. The *Enterprise* noted that "While the legal preliminaries were being arranged the Sherman Act was repealed and silver received its death blow." The newspaper further commented that with that action "went all hope of a railroad to Mogollon as well as the large amount of money already invested." Such setbacks were only temporary stumbling blocks for men like Newcomb. One way to make good was through forging good contacts. The segment of the railroad to Pinos Altos was built and actually operated for a few years in the early 1900s.

Networking was a characteristic of these early successful New Mexicans, and Newcomb was no exception. He was a brother-in-law of Howard H. Betts, also profiled in the *Optic Cartoon Book*. He was a "staunch Republican" and an active lodge member. Newcomb was both an "enthusiastic Elk" and a high ranking officer of the Masonic lodge throughout the territory. Furthermore, he was a member of the executive committee of the Territorial Republican Central Committee and for five years served on the Territorial Penitentiary Commission. He regularly rubbed shoulders with such men as Holm O. Burgum, one of the most powerful politicians in the territory. Sharing information to advance their business and political careers would have been commonplace and expected.

The *Enterprise* could not have summed up Newcomb's life any better. "His influence upon the development of this section of the Southwest was undeniably very great."

HON. MIGUEL A. OTERO,
SANTA FE

Miguel A. Otero: Politician and writer

Politician and writer. "Gillie" to his friends, "The little governor" to his detractors when he was in office. He accomplished things during his nearly eighty-five years that could (and did) fill a book (four of them). He was acquainted with everyone of his time worth knowing and many who were not. That was Miguel Antonio Otero, who could trace his lineage back to Old Castile although thoroughly American, having been born in St. Louis and attending Notre Dame.

Perhaps the best account of Otero's life, but obviously the most personal, comes from his own writing. The first two installments of his three-part autobiography *My Life on the Frontier* (1864–1882) and (1882–1897) are chock-full of incidents and characters he encountered during thirty-three years on the "ever receding" frontier of Missouri, Kansas, and Colorado before President William McKinley appointed him Governor of New Mexico in 1897 at just thirty-seven.

The story of his service in Santa Fe is related in *My Nine Years as Governor 1897–1906*. The *Two Lives* books include encounters with Western characters such as Kit Carson, Wild Bill Hickok, George Armstrong Custer, Doc Holiday, Bat Masterson, and of course, Billy the Kid. That is covered in a fourth book, *The Real Billy the Kid: With New Light on the Lincoln County War*. It is perhaps the only book to treat the youthful outlaw somewhat positively. Otero's books are "filled with the raw power and intrigue of the Wild West written by one who lived it," comments Ray John de Aragón in the foreword to the Sunstone Press edition of *My Life 1882–1897*.

There was nothing to hint at the adventuresome life Otero was to lead. He was born in St. Louis October 17, 1859, and attended college at St. Louis University and the University of Notre Dame where he displayed a proclivity for socializing over scholarship. Meanwhile, his businessman and railroad baron father had moved to Las Vegas, New Mexico, and the younger Otero followed to join his family in 1880. Young Otero had only dabbled at college.

Settling in Las Vegas, he first worked in his father's bank and then in land and livestock. Otero relates in his 1882–1887 memoirs that while on a business trip to Mexico some friends in Las Vegas "secured for me the Republican nomination for treasurer" and "This marked my entry into the political field." City and county offices followed one after another until his selection in 1892 as a delegate to the Republican National Convention in Minneapolis.

There occurred a fortuitous meeting with McKinley. The young Otero made a favorable impression on the Ohio senator. Seven years later, with some twenty contenders scrabbling for McKinley's nod as governor, the President picked Otero. He was then the youngest and the first of Spanish ancestry to be selected for the office by an American President. Although "a live wire," within four years he had gained the respect of imminent New Mexicans such as Ralph Emerson Twitchell. Twitchell told McKinley Otero was "the most capable, painstaking, worthy and dignified executive" the territory had ever had. Otero was twice appointed governor—first by McKinley again and then by President Theodore Roosevelt, who bowed to pressure and replaced him in 1906. But, as the Office of the State Historian has observed, "Nine years in office is a remarkable record for a Governor of New Mexico."

With service as Governor a relatively short span of Otero's life, it was natural that he would turn to other pursuits. He returned to banking and mining but found the lure of politics too strong and in 1909–1911 served as state treasurer. In 1912 he sought the governorship again but failed to secure the Republican nomination which went to Holm O. Bursum instead. He eventually became a Democrat and a supporter of President Woodrow Wilson. From 1917–1921 he was marshal of the Panama Canal.

Otero's life was so full of one adventure after another that it is difficult to select only one or two. In 1936 he published the Billy the Kid book based on a brief association with the outlaw in 1880. Otero and his brother Page rode with the prisoner while he was being transported by train from Las Vegas to Santa Fe for incarceration. The brothers visited the Kid in jail several times and supplied him with various creature comforts. They found the Kid agreeable company if not especially intellectually endowed.

Another incident concerned a confrontation in 1883 with the notorious Santa Fe Ring which Otero had branded as the "most corrupt, unscrupulous and daring organization" ever. It concerned the Ring's brazen attempts to steal the Otero family's Nuestra Senora de Los Delores mine in southern Santa Fe County. By his own admission, Otero was never reluctant to reach for a Colt or a Winchester or even to threaten use of a rope to defend his interests. Accordingly, Otero and an armed party seized the mine at gunpoint and then held off a gang sent by the Ring. The tense stand-off ended with Otero and his men jailed in Santa Fe for seven weeks before a jury trial and acquittal. The mine was eventually sold but Otero received nothing.

Otero's books make compelling reading. His life was one long adventure. He died August 7, 1944, in Santa Fe County and is interred at Fairview Cemetery in Santa Fe.

JUDGE FRANK W. PARKER.
LAS CRUCES

Frank W. Parker: High profile jurist, Chief Justice of the New Mexico Supreme Court

Of the three Las Crucens represented in the *Optic Cartoon Book* none was better known outside his city than Frank W. Parker. The Branigan Library of Las Cruces begins his write-up this way: "Judge Frank W. Parker gained state and national renown from his participation in two high profile, southern New Mexico trials." Succinct and accurate. Parker was also an Associate Justice and Chief Justice of the New Mexico Supreme Court.

Parker was another frontier New Mexican whose roots lay elsewhere. He arrived in the territory in 1881 soon after matriculating from the University of Michigan School of Law. His destination was Hillsboro, today a sleepy village in the Black Range, a way station for those traveling between Interstate 25 and Silver City but when Parker first saw it a roaring gold camp. Perhaps it was Hillsboro's lawlessness which attracted those who upheld the law.

In Hillsboro Parker met another young lawyer, Albert B. Fall, one among hundreds prospecting for gold and silver. It was natural that he and Parker would gravitate toward each other, educated men among the mostly unlettered. They were not to know they would become legal adversaries—one sitting upon the bench and the other pleading before it.

Fast forward almost two decades to near the turn of the century. By 1899 Parker was a territorial district judge conducting the trial of ranchers Oliver Lee and Jim Gilliland in the slaying/disappearance of lawyer and Republican stalwart Albert Jennings Fountain and his young son Henry. The pair had disappeared three years earlier. (Hamm 2012) Everything about the trial was sensational. Big names abounded, and the press clamored for news. Western Union, responding to demands from the Associated Press and the Hearst newspapers, ran a wire to the remote Hillsboro to help satisfy the need for coverage. Dona Ana County Sheriff Pat Garrett had pressed for Lee's and Gilliland's indictment. Garrett was someone also not included in the *Optic Cartoon Book* although he certainly merited inclusion if for no other reason than his notoriety as slayer of Billy the Kid. Big names, political shenanigans. It was all there in the trial.

Fall represented Lee. Thomas B. Catron was on the other side. Fall was out to win at all costs. Using his party connections, Fall contrived to have a new county created—Otero—so the proceedings would not be held in Dona Ana County. That venue had to be avoided because that was where all of the principals had once resided. A fair trial in Las Cruces was next to impossible. It all made for high drama.

Parker was equal to the task. He exhibited a propensity for high profile trials. As proceedings continued, one angry exchange occurred when Fall became increasingly aggressive. According to Gordon R. Owen in *The Two Alberts: Fountain and Fall*, "The prosecution of Oliver Lee is the result of a conspiracy to send an innocent man to the gallows. The district attorney is involved in that conspiracy; the Honorable Thomas B. Catron is involved in that conspiracy. His honor on the bench is involved in that conspiracy."

The challenge could not be ignored. Parker warned Fall to withdraw his remarks or face contempt. Did the defense attorney want to go to jail? The judicial bickering continued. One motion followed another. Owen sets the scene. Parker ordered the jury sequestered for the night. Fall demanded that deliberations begin immediately. Parker acceded. It took the jury all of ten minutes to find Lee and Gilliland not guilty. Fall had won, but Parker would go down in territorial annals as the man who conducted the trial.

Another equally well known proceeding was to follow in a decade. Ten years after the Lee-Gilliland trial, Parker was again front and center on the judicial stage. He conducted the trial. This time Garrett was the victim. Wayne Brazil had been charged with his murder. Again Fall was in the corner for the defense. Again he secured an acquittal. Parker was to continue on the bench for many more years, but no other trial he was to conduct matched these two for headline-grabbing attention.

Parker played a key role at the 1910 New Mexico Constitutional Convention, chairing the judicial committee. One key amendment called for extending terms of Supreme Court judges from six to eight years. It passed handily. Old Guard Republicans favored an elected judiciary. The *New Mexico Law Review* ("The Birth of a Partisan Judiciary 1910–1911") notes that Parker "played an inordinately influential role in drafting the article as finally adopted." It was, the *Review* article continued, "more than mere coincidence that he served on the Supreme Court (from his election November 7, 1911) until his death in 1932." Ralph Emerson Twitchell wrote that several of Parker's opinions, especially those dealing with mining and irrigation law, were "legal classics, having set precedents" upheld by the United States Supreme Court.

Parker was also instrumental in construction of the Elephant Butte reservoir, near where he owned a large farm. He also played a prominent role in founding what is now New Mexico State University in Las Cruces, according to Twitchell.

Death came August 3, 1932. Parker's gavel was stilled forever at age seventy one.

F. H. PIERCE, ESQ.
LAS VEGAS

Frederick H. Pierce: Active in the business life of Las Vegas

When Kentucky native Frederick H. Pierce relocated to Las Vegas in 1886, he immediately immersed himself in the life of his new community and quickly assumed a dominant role in its business affairs. Moving to Las Vegas to assume management of the Agua Pura Ice Company, he was soon elected the company's secretary-treasurer.

Pierce was "prominent in assisting every enterprise which has been promoted in the interests of Las Vegas," reported the *Las Vegas Optic* in its February 17, 1906, edition. Those activities ranged from negotiating the location of the National Fraternal Sanitarium to Las Vegas to serving as a director of the Las Vegas Land Grant. He was also president of the Commercial Club, and according to the *Breckenridge News* in his native Kentucky, was "always known to bend every effort" to promote the growth of Las Vegas.

Positions with other business enterprises included president of the Investment and Agency Corporation, vice president and treasurer of the Douglas Avenue Building Company, director and treasurer of the Mutual Improvement Company, and treasurer of the Las Vegas Tent Company.

He was also active outside the realm of business. Non-business positions of leadership included serving as treasurer of the Las Vegas Driving Park and Fair Association, serving as trustee of the Presbyterian Church, and serving four terms on the Territorial Penitentiary Board.

He died February 24, 1912, in Owensboro, Kentucky, at age fifty-four.

W. C. PORTERFIELD, Esq.,
SILVER CITY

William C. Porterfield: Pharmacist, solider, important turquoise figure

William C. Porterfield brought with him an important attribute to New Mexico when he arrived in 1887: professional experience in pharmacy. He soon added two more qualities: a keen interest in turquoise along with his brother M.W. Porterfield and a desire to defend his new homeland. With backgrounds in drugstore ownership in their native Illinois and ownership of pharmacies throughout the Midwest, he and his brother were also soon caught up in turquoise mining. But with Poncho Villa's raid on Columbus, in 1916, William C. Porterfield soon had another vocation—the military.

Because of his desire to serve and protect, Porterfield helped organize the First New Mexico Infantry Regiment of the National Guard. He participated in General "Black Jack" Pershing's incursion into Mexico in pursuit of Villa. When the Guard was transferred into the Army's 40th Division, he saw service in World War I. After seventeen years of combined service, he reached the age of mandatory retirement. Porterfield put aside his uniform and with it the rank of lieutenant colonel. Pharmacy was his profession and his livelihood, but turquoise was his passion.

When the Legislature enacted the Territorial Pharmacy Act of 1889 which he helped draft, Porterfield was a logical choice for appointment to the New Mexico Board of Pharmacy by Governor E.G. Ross. He later served as secretary and treasurer. What else beckoned? Military service and drug store ownership had not been enough.

Like others before them in southwestern New Mexico, Porterfield and his brother engaged in mining. But while others sought silver and gold; the Porterfields sought precious gemstones. They organized the Porterfield Turquoise Mines Company and are credited for having rediscovered the stone in Grant County and then promoting it. In 1907 *History of New Mexico* noted that M.W. Porterfield "may be considered the father of turquoise mining...in New Mexico, if not in the United States." "The Turquoise King," as he was known, headed mineral exhibits at major expositions of the time, including the Chicago Exposition in 1893 and the Louisiana Purchase Exposition in St. Louis in 1904. The St. Louis exhibit, which included a dummy mine, attracted big crowds. It demonstrated that turquoise from New Mexico's Burro Mountains is "by far the most superior in quality of any seen throughout the United States," reported the *Silver City Independent* of August 23, 1905. Such efforts help recognize Porterfield's standing among mineralogists of the day. At one time, the brothers' mines supplied nearly three-fourths of all turquoise sold worldwide. Still mining was not enough.

Like so many in the *Optic Cartoon Book*, Porterfield was a committed Republican at the territorial and national levels. He represented the territory at President Willard Howard Taft's inauguration. In 1920 he was a delegate to the National Convention, which nominated Warren G. Harding as president. He was a 32nd degree Mason, an officer of the Elks lodge, and active in the American Legion.

A pioneer in pharmacy. A military leader. A promoter of turquoise. "A firm adherent to the principles of justice and right." (Haines1891) When William C. Porterfield died January 14, 1943, at eighty-four he had been those things.

HON. GEORGE W. PRITCHARD,
SANTA FE

George W. Prichard: Jurist, orator, mining man

When George W. Prichard died in Santa Fe February 15, 1935, at age eighty-four he had fulfilled the promise of his early private education by tutors in New Harmony, Indiana, provided by a father who envisioned great things for his son. The young Prichard graduated in law from the University of Michigan in 1872. Soon after he began practice in Little Rock, Arkansas. There he cast his first Republican presidential electoral ballot in 1876 for Rutherford B. Hayes. He voted for no fewer than fifteen presidential candidates during his lifetime. Like so many before him, he came west to restore his health. Prichard found himself in New Mexico Territory in 1879 and there the mining fever struck.

Prichard compiled a long record of public service. He was elected twice to the Territorial Council. There, the *Las Vegas Optic* noted, he compiled a record of "honesty and carefulness." He participated in the New Mexico Constitutional Convention where he chaired the education committee, drafting a number of important proposals.

He was appointed United States Attorney General for New Mexico by President Chester A. Arthur and then Attorney General for New Mexico by Governor Miguel A. Otero. He had campaigned for Otero in 1904, speaking for him in all but a handful of counties. On the stump, as an attorney, or on the bench, he was always known as "a man of eloquence." But mining was an abiding interest.

For a number of years Prichard lived in White Oaks. He acquired stock in gold mines near Carrizozo. He devoted much of his time to mining, building mills for processing ore and practicing mining law. He was a member of the New Mexico Bar Association for more than twenty-five years.

After moving to Santa Fe upon becoming Attorney General Prichard and his wife were known as lavish entertainers and patrons of the arts. In commenting upon his death the *Santa Fe New Mexican* called him one of the "unterrified" for living through the territory's days of outlawry. Until his last days, the newspaper wrote, Prichard "retained a fine carriage, a sparkling eye and a rich voice to the end."

R. C. RANKIN, ESQ.
LAS VEGAS

Robert C. Rankin: Citizen solider, Indian trader, lawmaker

Robert C. Rankin was a citizen soldier when the term did not carry today's meaning as merely a recruiting slogan but rather entailed the concept of one's service to country and state. He exemplified the ideal. Throughout his long life he was a railroad man, an Indian trader, a Wells Fargo agent, an insurance broker, and a banker. During it all, he remained constant to the idea of military service as a civilian.

Born March 29, 1866, Rankin was a graduate of the University of Kansas, where he held a unique position in university athletics. He captained Kansas's only rowing team, which trained one year on the Kaw River. He took "gap years" off between public schooling and his university degree to serve as a page in the 47th and 48th United States Congresses and to trade with the native people in the Indian Territory of Oklahoma. There he ran a trading post owned by his father, colonel John K. Rankin. He then began several years employment in railroading, first with the Southern Kansas Railway, then with the Santa Fe in Topeka, and finally at Guthrie, Oklahoma, in 1888.

After a brief period in insurance, Rankin joined the Wells Fargo Company serving as an agent for that firm in Colorado Springs, Pueblo, Denver, and Albuquerque before a final transfer to Las Vegas. After four years he left Wells Fargo to begin a career with the San Miguel Bank of Las Vegas.

During his various positions he was actively involved with the National Guard in Kansas, Colorado, and New Mexico. In the New Mexico Territory he was a lieutenant colonel in the First Infantry. He resigned that rank to organize a cavalry squadron. When the Spanish-American War broke out he opened a Rough Riders recruiting office in Las Vegas. He was so successful that he was asked to furnish an additional fifteen volunteers. Poor health, however, prohibited him from taking part in active service. However, he was involved with the Rough Riders Society throughout his life. His name was in the territorial newspapers on several occasions in connection with his military duties until on October 31, 1907 the *Albuquerque Citizen* ran a brief item announcing that he had been relieved of duty by order of the Adjutant General of the Territory.

Meanwhile, he still found time to participate in the community service life of Las Vegas. He was instrumental in pushing for construction of a concrete sidewalk system for the city, chaired the City Council, and served as chairman of the San Miguel County Commission. He was a Republican and a Mason.

After serving as treasurer of a new railroad in California, he returned to Las Vegas to see New Mexico admitted as a state. In 1912 he returned to Lawrence. Back home he managed the family ice and cold storage business for thirty-five years, served as mayor of Lawrence from 1927–1930, and served in the Kansas Legislature eight years, four in each chamber. He was president of the Kansas Historical Society 1938–1939 and was serving on the executive committee at the time of his death. His contributions to the society are noted in the *Kansas Historical Quarterly, Volume 22, Issue 1, 1956*. He died in Lawrence on September 25, 1954, at age eighty-eight

SECRETARY J. W. RAYNOLDS
SANTA FE

James W. Raynolds: He exercised the Wisdom of Solomon

James W. Raynolds had been Acting Governor of New Mexico less than a week in the spring of 1907 when he was confronted with a problem that would ultimately call for the Wisdom of Solomon. In the end, he made an inspired decision in one of the territory's most controversial murder trials. His solution, as the Office of the State Historian has noted and from which this account is drawn, was "a masterful example of political expediency and legal logic." The contretemps was the infamous Hillsboro murder case in which two sixteen-year-old girls had been convicted and sentenced to hang in the arsenic poisoning of Manuel Madrid, who had died an excruciating death the morning of March 30, 1907.

Nothing in Raynolds' professional life had prepared him for dealing with the matter's complexities and attendant issues. The case attracted national attention. Nothing came close to matching the notoriety attached to it. Raynolds simply had no preparation. He was thirty-four. He was a graduate of the Massachusetts Institute of Technology with no legal training. What Raynolds did have going for him, however, as the *Las Vegas Optic* had observed just a year before, was the "ability and sagacity of a man of years." Those qualities were to be tested to the limit. They proved to be enough.

The backstory is necessary. Valentina Madrid was the deceased's wife despite their wide disparity in age. Her friend, Alma Lyons, a "colored girl," was the same age. When Dr. Frank I. Given examined Madrid as he lay dying he found signs of arsenic poisoning so obvious that "the merest novice in medicine" would have spotted them. Cornered as they were, the pair quickly gave up accomplice Francisco Baca, Madrid's alleged lover.

Raynolds' preparation was not a fit for dealing with what was to come. He had entered MIT in 1889 and earned a degree in mining engineering. Three years later he was working in the First National Bank of Las Vegas. His next career move was public service. When George H. Wallace was appointed Secretary of the Territory Raynolds accompanied him to Santa Fe as assistant secretary. Upon Wallace's death in 1901 President William McKinley named him to fill the unexpired term. President Theodore Roosevelt subsequently appointed Raynolds for a full four-year term and then again for another.

Ralph Emerson Twitchell has asserted that the office of secretary of the territory was "the most lucrative" in New Mexico. He claims Herbert J. Hagerman made "a serious mistake" in retaining Raynolds in that position because what the governor really needed was someone "in whom he could repose entire political confidence." Apparently he did not have that in Raynolds. Raynolds assumed the duties of acting governor following Hagerman's resignation on May 3, 1907. The stage was set for the biggest role of his young life.

The Hillsboro case created a sensation. The girls' age, the alleged affair between Baca and the young widow, and the grisly aspects of her husband's death put the spotlight squarely upon the girls, upon Hillsboro, upon New Mexico, and upon Raynolds. No one relished it. All three defendants appeared before District Judge Frank W. Parker in May of 1907. All entered not guilty pleas. Judge Parker ruled that Baca could separate his case from the others. Francisco Baca was quickly shunted off to the territorial penitentiary for "safe keeping" to await his turn in the dock. District Attorney H.A. Wolford appointed Elfego Baca of Frisco Shootout fame as special prosecutor. Baca did his job. On May 9 the jury took less than an hour to find the girls guilty of murder in the first degree.

The next morning the pair appeared for sentencing. They admitted their part but insisted Baca conceived the plan and threatened to kill them if they did not accede. The judge heard them out. He then administered the only sentence then permitted: death by hanging on June 7. "I am sorry for you," the judge told the defendants. "It is a duty which I would escape if there were any way for me to do," he intoned.

Judge Parker's sentence put Raynolds in a most uncomfortable position. Newspapers around the territory quickly weighed in. Most favored executive clemency. A few called for the full measure of the law to be exacted. Meanwhile, Raynolds was receiving petitions and letters pointing to the girls' mental deficiency and claiming that to execute them would be "like hanging children." He took advice from grayer heads than his around the territory, listening to all, and weighing their counsel. Finally, Raynolds announced his decision: executing the girls, he said, would eliminate the only witnesses against Baca. Their age and mental incompetence did not factor in his decision, he said. Raynolds was off the hook.

After many delays and postponed trials, a jury found that, while Baca influenced the girls and was an accomplice to murder, there was not enough evidence to convict him of first degree murder. He went free. The girls were returned to Santa Fe and continued serving their sentence until Governor O. A. Larrazolo on March 3, 1920, commuted their sentence to time served. A few days later, the prison gates swung open for them.

Raynolds did not live to see the end of the saga. He died in 1910.

JOSHUA S. RAYNOLDS, ESQ.,
ALBUQUERQUE

Joshua S. Raynolds: He had an imprint on three cities, was McNary's mentor

Joshua S. Raynolds helped found a banking dynasty. He was influential in the business and civic life of Las Vegas, Albuquerque, and El Paso, where a downtown street bears his name. He guided the transition of son-in-law James G. McNary from newspaper publishing to the financial world. His name was synonymous with good works. However, he saw it all collapse around him during the Depression.

Raynolds, along with brothers Frederick and Jefferson, all of Canton, Ohio, first moved west to Central City, Colorado, where they entered banking. In Canton Raynolds and his brothers counted as their close friend William McKinley, who became President of the United States in 1897. They continued the banking profession in Las Vegas. In 1878 the Territory of New Mexico granted them a charter for The Central Bank. They opened under that name in Albuquerque.

In 1881 the Central Bank merged with the First National Bank of Albuquerque. The institution stood for stability until the calamitous events culminating in its closure on April 15, 1933. Its failure had not been entirely unexpected, says William A. Keleher in *New Mexicans I Knew: Memoirs, 1892-1969*. He writes that the Raynolds empire began to disintegrate when in early September 1931 the First National Bank of El Paso closed "despite the heroic efforts" of James G. McNary. McNary had entered banking after editing and publishing the *Las Vegas Optic*, where he brought out the *Optic Cartoon Book*.

Raynolds believed in giving back to the cities where he did business. In 1896 he purchased a former school building in downtown Albuquerque and gave it to the city as a municipal free library so long as a facility be built there, that the city maintain the grounds, and that residents raise $1000 in matching funds. (Albuquerque Libraries: It's a Grand Old History)

Sadly, not all of Raynolds' buildings served such uplifting purposes or fared as well. The First National Bank of El Paso was built in the Second Empire Style with Italianate details in

1882–1883 in anticipation of a boom created by location of the railroad in that city, but it fell into disuse after the bank failed in 1933. According to a Historic American Buildings Survey in the late 1990s, the building then housed a jewelry store and a shop selling pornographic items.

Although Raynolds was compelled to utilize attorneys he did not completely trust their motives. William Keleher relates a story told by the minister of the Presbyterian Church Raynolds attended. An attorney wrote the clergyman asking about prospects in Albuquerque. Raynolds told the minister to ask the attorney one question: "Would he be willing to sue another lawyer and get judgment against him on a promissory note?" Apparently, according to Keleher, Raynolds had been upset more than once by "professional courtesy" extended from one member of the bar to another. "He could not collect the bank's money on notes which lawyers had signed" and had about concluded that "Albuquerque lawyers had entered into a conspiracy not to sue each other."

Raynolds was born December 31, 1845, just in time to see service in the Civil War as a sergeant with the 162nd Regiment of the Ohio Volunteer Infantry. The *Las Vegas Optic* lauded Raynolds by writing that his name "stands for stability, good business methods, good management, and absolute honesty."

HON. A. B. RENEHAN,
SANTA FE

A.B. Renehan: A zealous worker for his clients and his party

Alois (A.B.) Renehan launched himself into his clients' affairs and politics with vigor and intensity from his very first day upon arrival in the New Mexico Territory on September 10, 1892, at age twenty-three. He never ceased in his labors or his devotion to either. Known for his intense work habits, passersby would frequently see him burning the midnight oil (there was no electricity yet), through his office windows in the Renehan Building on the Santa Fe Plaza. His labors were such that he reportedly suffered from a nervous breakdown and was ordered to rest in Florida for the winter of 1927. This advice he followed but died April 20, 1928, in a Dayton, Ohio, hospital on his way home to Santa Fe. He was fifty nine. He had literally worked himself to death.

Aloysius, who had shortened his name to Alois thinking the abbreviated version would be easier to pronounce for the town's Hispanic majority, had left his family and vocation behind in the East. His family's success might have presaged his own. Alois's father had been an associate editor under Horace Greeley at the *New York Tribune*. Alois's grandfather, Martin, had immigrated to America in the 1830s and through dint of hard work and good luck, landed a good job at the White House. Despite a thick Irish brogue, he became a doorkeeper at the White House when that post was a position of considerable authority and influence. He retained it through four administrations. "It was quite an influential post," says Edward Renehan." Martin Renehan was both doorman and doorkeeper. No one could see the president without his say so." Alois Renehan had moved to the Washington area to continue his education. His reasons for leaving Virginia behind were clear enough; his choice of New Mexico was not but it proved fortuitous.

Renehan quickly gained admission to the New Mexico Bar and soon became engaged in private practice, including divorce cases. In 1895, a year after beginning practice, he was appointed city attorney and served until 1898. He represented many well-known clients over the course of his long career. There were at least three with some degree of notoriety. One of his most colorful clients was Charles Siringo, the "Cowboy Detective." Siringo was a rancher and Pinkerton Man who in the course of his work encountered such diverse personalities as Billy the Kid and Clarence Darrow. Another locally famous client was Renehan's second wife. His best known client, however, was United States Senator Holm O. Bursum, who often sought his counsel.

There were at least two well-known known instances of this. One was in seeking Renehan's assistance in drafting Bursum's Pueblo Lands Bill. Bursum biographer Donald R. Moorman says newspapers throughout the country questioned the "political and moral integrity" of every Republican associated with the measure. (Hamm 2012) To many, the bill was just a land grab in another guise; to others it was a well-intentioned attempt to clarify legislation affecting Pueblo Indians. The measure was as complicated as it was controversial. Some observers even assert the bill cost Bursum his re-election contest against Judge Sam Bratton in the 1924 election. That was the second time Renehan came to his well-known client's aid.

Bursum lost no time in asserting his claim and Renehan was in the forefront. This is attested to in the voluminous correspondence between the two over the course of the challenge and the many trips Renehan made to Washington to plead before the Senate upon his client's behalf and his appearances before the Legislature in Santa Fe. The senator claimed he had lost by less than 3,000 votes. Renehan told the Senate Committee on Privileges and Elections that the *Clovis News Journal* had expressed the hope in its November 16, 1924, edition that the Democrats "actually stole the election and were able to conceal their tracks." (Hamm 2012)

Renehan made one last-ditch effort before the Committee on April 22, 1926, when he charged that "I confess that I am in a fog and I am inclined to think the committee is in a fog, or more properly in a bog, because of the changes in procedure adopted in the middle of the stream. ...While we traveled along this appointed road in confidence because we were told it was safe, we have been shot at, if not struck, from ambush." Such rhetoric, even if accurate, did little to advance his client's cause.

The law was only one dimension to Renehan's busy professional life. In 1900 he organized the New Mexico Realty Syndicate and soon followed with ventures in banking. The following year he assumed control of the Capital City Bank of Santa Fe. All the while, he combined business activities with those in the civic arena. In 1913 he was president of the Santa Fe Chamber of Commerce. Politics were never very far from his mind. He was a member of the school board and president of the City Council. On June 20, 1910, writes Ralph Emerson Twitchell in *Leading Facts of New Mexican History*, "(a) firm belief in the cause of protection for American industries" led Renehan to switch parties. He became a Republican. Thus a man who had chaired the Territorial Democratic Central Committee and who had twice represented New Mexico at Democratic national conventions eventually was to be elected as a Republican to the New Mexico House of Representatives.

Despite his hectic already overloaded work schedule Renehan was always on the lookout for additional clients. On March 24, 1919, he wrote Bursum soliciting the position of Delinquent Tax Attorney. While acknowledging the post would entail much work, he promised he would "handle its affairs with energy and exclusive attention" if given the post. Renehan added that even though he had never sought political favors he was always ready "to serve at command."

Although Renehan always threw himself into his legal practice he was known as an orator and raconteur with a large arsenal of jokes as might be expected of an Irishman whose people are known for their love of stories and storytelling. He also was a published poet. His *Songs from the Black Mesa*, published in 1901, is still available from Amazon Books.

Renehan's restless mind ranged far afield from his legal work. The *Santa Fe New Mexican* on November 13, 1909, reported that the United States Patent Office had granted Renehan a patent for a "bath cabinet" to give dry heat baths. The contrivance was designed to be attached to a steam or hot water heating system. If neither was present, it could be hooked up to a hot water faucet. There was no report on how successful the contraption was or whether Renehan realized any profits from it. Renehan did not confine such interests to mere tinkering.

Renehan liked gadgets, especially fast handsome ones that eased his life. On July 14,

1908, the *New Mexican* reported that he had "joined the ranks of the automobile enthusiasts by investing in a handsome four-cylinder Ford Model roadster." Renehan, the newspaper noted, was "getting next to its intricate workings" under the "professional tutelage" of chauffeur and local Ford agent Earl Mayes. Renehan would thus be able to travel "to and from his beautiful home, 'The Willows,'" conveniently and in style. The Renehans had moved into it upon their marriage in 1909.

As with any well-known personage, legends sometimes grow up in the shadow of death. Renehan is no exception. Of those, the most intriguing is the tale of the so-called "black kiss." Descendent Edward Renehan relates that there is a life-sized kiss in black on Renehan's mausoleum. If one knows where to look, he says, the kiss can be spotted on the right side of the doorway of the tomb. While his story cannot be verified, there are many aspects to Renehan's life that can.

Successful as he later was, Renehan early on did many things that soured relationships with his family and incurred its displeasure. Initially, he abandoned his priestly studies. Secondly, he married outside his faith to Jewess Zeporah Gold whom he subsequently divorced. Thirdly, he wed a second time to a divorcée whom he had represented in a headline-grabbing case, and lastly he deserted the Democratic Party, his family's lifelong political affiliation, to become a Republican.

When Alois died, his remains were placed in Thomas B. Catron's mausoleum at Fairview Cemetery in Santa Fe until his could be built. When Governor Arthur Seligman died in 1932 his remains were placed in the Renehan mausoleum until his sarcophagus could be constructed. Thus the family jokes that Catron, Renehan, and Seligman all slept together.

Twitchell summed up Renehan this way: "(H)is position is never...equivocal. He stands fearlessly and loyally for what he believes to be right."

CLEOFAS ROMERO, ESQ.
LAS VEGAS

Cleofes Romero: Three-time sheriff of San Miguel County

One of two Romero brothers of Las Vegas who spent their careers in law enforcement and government, Cleofes Romero was a three-time sheriff of San Miguel County. He also served his county as deputy sheriff, deputy clerk, and deputy treasurer. The *Las Vegas Optic* lauded the veteran lawman for a "high type of personal bravery...entirely free from bravado." One of his headline achievements, the newspaper said, was capturing six cattle rustlers who had been depleting the herds of an area ranch, defying other lawmen and the cattlemen themselves to bring them to justice.

Cleofes Romero's time in office was not entirely free of criticism. During territorial times, New Mexico's county jails would sometimes house federal prisoners and were sometimes lax or slipshod in their supervision. In the fall of 1901 United States Marshal Creighton M. Foraker chided Romero for allowing federal prisoners "too much liberty." Larry D. Ball in *The United States Marshals of New Mexico and Arizona Territories 1846–1912* writes that Foraker once complained of such dereliction to United States Attorney General William H. Moody. "I think that they (the prisoners) have become too familiar with their keepers," he charged, adding that, "The jailer has taken them out of their jail and into saloons...."

Romero knew something of the marshal's office. He had prepared for his time as sheriff by serving as a Deputy U.S. Marshal during the tumultuous times of the Las Gorras Blancas (white caps), local Spanish-American activists who rose up against Anglo encroachment on their lands around Las Vegas. They tore down fences and scattered cattle and burned barns. After leaving the sheriff's office, Romero in 1910 became Superintendent of the New Mexico Penitentiary. He then entered private business

Cleofes and his wife joined with his father Eugenio to establish sawmills and general stores in in the forested areas east of the Sandia and Manzano Mountains around Albuquerque where timber could be utilized in new railroad construction in the area. After he returned home to Las Vegas, one of Romero's last public appearances was as an "elder" in the 1933 Historical Society Biennial Celebration in Las Vegas. He was born September 24, 1865, in Las Vegas and died April 5, 1949, in Las Vegas.

HON. EUGENIO ROMERO,
LAS VEGAS

Eugenio Romero: Patriarch of a powerful political family

Don Eugenio Romero was a successful man in his own right as merchant, freighter, and businessman. He also sired two politically powerful sons. Together they ran Las Vegas for some seventy years, says Las Vegas attorney and historian Jesus L. Lopez. "For almost seven decades," writes Lopez, "one family would dominate the social, financial and political landscape of Las Vegas and San Miguel County."

Eugenio Romero descended from one of the great Spanish families of New Mexico. His great grandfather was born in Spain, and his grandfather was born in Mexico City. Eugenio was born November 15, 1837, in La Cienega south of Santa Fe. His father was one of the first settlers of Las Vegas and was a trustee of the Las Vegas Land Grant.

With such a pedigree the Romeros of Las Vegas were certain to prosper, and prosper they did. As soon as he was able, Eugenio entered the freighting business on the nearby Old Santa Fe Trail and went on to parlay that into mercantile stores, lumber yards, and stock grazing.

With a firm financial base, Eugenio felt secure enough to enter politics. He soon held a succession of elective posts. He began in the New Mexico House of Representatives in 1860, as sheriff and collector of San Miguel County from 1879–1881, as county assessor from 1881–1883, as mayor of Las Vegas from 1882–1886, in the Territorial Senate in 1899, as San Miguel county treasurer and collector from 1903–1911, as coal oil inspector from 1905–1907, as a member of the executive committee of the Republican Central Committee, and finally as the first treasurer and collector for San Miguel County under state government in 1912. He was also first chief of the East Romero Hose & Fire Company.

Here is how Lopez described the power and influence of the Romero family in a column for the *Las Vegas Optic*:

"The sons of this Las Vegas dynasty would help ensure that New Mexico was admitted to the Union.

"They would represent our town (Las Vegas) and county (San Miguel) in Santa Fe at the constitutional convention in 1910, and there ensure that New Mexico's constitution would forever protect the rights of Hispanic New Mexicans.

"They would serve as our U.S. marshals and long-time mayors of Las Vegas and sheriffs of San Miguel County, would establish our first fire department, and provide the first buildings for our courts and government offices.

"They would establish great mercantile houses, build the Plaza Hotel and erect the most elegant mansions in all the southwest.

"They would provide the financial wherewithal to establish the first formal educational system in Las Vegas, and would care for the disabled and mentally ill and ensure that New Mexico's state hospital was located here (Las Vegas).

"This was the great Romero family, and they ruled supreme."

Don Eugenio died September 30, 1920.

SEGUNDINO ROMERO, Esq.
LAS VEGAS

Secundino Romero: Republican Party power broker, *patron*

Secundino Romero was a consummate politician and Republican Party power broker. Some of his influence came through ownership of *El Independiente*, one of the most successful Spanish-language newspapers of its time. But most of it was attained through the various political offices he held. If a political issue affected his city, his county, or the territory Secundino Romero was sure to be at the heart of it attempting to sway the outcome his way.

The *Las Vegas Optic* wrote that he "possesses a genial disposition, an engaging manner, and a strong personality." Political opponents certainly would have felt the force of that engaging personality. One also wonders what the *Optic* had in mind in referring to Romero as possessing "a genial disposition" because Larry D. Ball, who writes about Western lawmen, says he had a "reputation for fractiousness." Ball was referring to an undated article in the *Albuquerque Evening Herald* in which its reporter termed Romero the "noted pugilist from San Miguel County" for his alleged assault against a judge.

"Sec" Romero, son of Don Eugenio Romero and brother of Cleofes Romero, was a force to be reckoned with. Many have called him a "boss." He has not always been treated sympathetically by his chroniclers. This master politician was many things, but politics was in his blood. Las Vegas attorney and historian Jesus L. Lopez calls him the "last of the Las Vegas patrons."

As sheriff of San Miguel County Romero bore "the ultimate badge of power," Lopez explains, because when he was sheriff there was no New Mexico State Police or FBI. "He was judge, jury, and prosecutor," Lopez continues. "Law enforcement was the Romero family business (Cleofes was also a sheriff)," notes Rob Dean in *Santa Fe: Its 400th year*. "Political power was its weapon of choice. (H)e and his brother also spent sixteen years in Santa Fe flashing their badges." They effectively traded the sheriff's job back and forth between them when they were not engaged in other aspects of law enforcement.

Romero's life began conventionally enough. Born July 1, 1869, he received an early Jesuit education and then attended St. Mary's College in Kansas. He had some formal business schooling and worked for two years as bookkeeper in large wholesale houses in Kansas City. Following that preparation, he returned to Las Vegas to work in the Romero & Romero family mercantile business. There he became active in Republican politics, including a term as mayor of Las Vegas and then Speaker of the New Mexico House of Representatives in 1915. His life was not all politics but mostly so. Romero found time to serve with the El Romero Hose Company for more than twenty years and belonged to the Elks, the Redmen, and the Knights of Pythias.

He played pivotal roles time and time again in the machinations of his party. One was in connection with Holm O. Bursum's nomination as the Republican candidate for governor in 1911. When it became clear Bursum had secured the nomination Romero instructed his seventy-five votes go to the Socorran, thus making the vote unanimous. "In a flash," reported the *Santa Fe New Mexican*, the Las Vegas's Duncan Opera House convention floor erupted and the place became a madhouse. (Hamm)

Equally important was another test of wills concerning the renomination prospects of President William H. Taft at the 1912 Republican National Convention as well as for another phase of Romero's political career. It came about with Taft's desire to retain Creighton M. Foraker (with whom Romero had earlier worked as clerk of the Fourth Judicial Court) as United States Marshal. Republican powerhouse Solomon Luna would have none of it. He "steadfastly demanded" Romero's appointment, writes Ball in the *United States Marshals of New Mexico and Arizona Territories 1846–1912*.

Luna let it be known, none too subtly, that only through Romero's appointment to the marshalcy could he Luna guarantee Taft "a solid pro administration delegation" to the convention and thus the President's nomination for a second term. That eventuality was too fearful for Taft to contemplate. Ralph Emerson Twitchell observes much the same in *Leading Facts of New Mexican History*. Romero's nomination made "a combination possible which otherwise could have been effected to the interest of the national administration."

Not all of Romero's battles occurred within the political realm although they were certainly closely connected with it. One concerned his sparring with Carl Magee, owner of the *Albuquerque State Tribune*. ("New Mexico's Man for All Seasons: Judge Luis Armijo of Las Vegas, *New Mexico*," (*New Mexico*) *Bar Journal* May/June 1996) The trouble erupted when Magee called San Miguel County "Sec Romero's empire" (which it probably was) and his political organization "a copper riveted machine." Fourth Judicial District Judge David Leahy was a close political ally of Romero's. They took offense at Magee's remarks, which were expanded to disparage the university and mental hospital, Las Vegas symbols of pride.

Eventually, Magee was arrested and forcibly removed to Las Vegas. He was found guilty of libel and contempt of court, but Governor James Hinkle pardoned him of all charges. The fallout continued beyond the trial, however, with lasting damaging results to the Romero machine. Magee's life was threatened, and Sheriff Lorenzo Delgado and then District Attorney Armijo intervened to protect him. That got them tossed out of Romero's organization. In 1924 they ran again for public office: Delgado for sheriff and Armijo for district judge. Their election "effectively destroyed the Romero machine in San Miguel County." (*Bar Journal*) Another aftermath occurred in a Las Vegas hotel lobby brawl in August of 1925 between Leahy and Magee. Leahy was wounded and an innocent bystander who tried to break up the fight was killed.

Romero died at age sixty August 20, 1929, at his 10,000 sheep and cattle ranch at El Cuervo, seventy-five miles south of Las Vegas. He is buried at Mount Calvary Cemetery in Las Vegas.

HUGO SEABERG, Esq.,
RATON

Hugo Seaberg: Hotel man, capitalist, speculator, risk taker

Hugo Seaberg came to America at eighteen determined to find his fortune in the New World. Find it he did because "his optimism never lagged behind his aspiration." However, the Great Depression and a penchant for overextension in his financial affairs ultimately spelled his downfall. Seaberg died a broken man in his seventh-fifth year but not before accumulating great wealth and influence, only to lose it all.

Seaberg, writes Meldon J. Preusser in a master's thesis for the University of Denver upon which this profile is based, founded his life on the principles of optimism, hard work, speculation, and risk taking. Seaberg was born in Bornholm, Sweden, December 15, 1869. But a poor economic climate and mandatory military inscription in his native country caused Seaberg to migrate to the United States, first to Chicago and then to Springer, New Mexico. There he was to come under the influence of prominent attorney and land owner Melvin W. Mills. Mills was to change Seaberg's life forever.

Under Mills Seaberg instituted personal and professional practices that were to remain with him throughout his life. When Mills gave Seaberg a list of duties for the day, for example, the younger man typed a memorandum for himself "that I may remember it, that I may read it over every morning and see if there is anything left to be done." Menial outdoor chores soon morphed into inside clerical work, which led to a study of the law.

Of his benefactor and tutor, Seaberg wrote: "I must say that Mr. Mills has helped me very much, and I am very thankful to him." Seaberg applied himself assiduously to his duties and his studies. On April 17, 1889, he signed a three-year contract with Mills, thus setting himself on his life's work of law. Possibilities for enhanced cash flow were always uppermost in the young man's mind—selling trees, cattle feed, periodical subscriptions, and Swedish stoves, anything that could turn a profit, extending even to running a mail route. When he entered the insurance business Seaberg asserted to potential clients that he had always attended "strictly to business and (had) no bad habits whatever."

The year 1893 marked several milestones for Seaberg. On May 20, he became a citizen and was admitted to the New Mexico Bar. He also married Lottie Mills. By the late 1890s Seaberg was a fixture in New Mexico financial circles. Soon another man was to come into Seaberg's life who was to play a major role in his further professional development. Denver financier Henry M. Porter owned substantial property in Springer, and he and Seaberg soon became acquaintances and then business associates.

About this time, according to Preusser, Seaberg began exhibiting a proclivity for "a daring and innovative fiscal policy" which would mark his investment strategies the rest of his life. This did not always have fortuitous outcomes. Acting on his optimism in the "steady growth of the economy," Seaberg began borrowing substantial amounts of cash from Eastern banks at low interest rates to facilitate large investments. This, Preusser notes, established a pattern of "relying upon loaned capital" for business expansion. The policy worked so long as the economy was sound. It became disastrous with the advent of the Depression.

Seaberg soon exhibited a propensity for two grand ventures: dealing in land script and plowing money into his beloved Hotel Seaberg in Raton, the city where he moved in 1903 when Springer became too small for his vision and ambition. In just a few years Seaberg had become one of the best known script dealers in the Southwest. When Seaberg was involved in the practice the term land script referred to a written claim of "lieu of land rights" offered by the government to railroads for facilitating right-of-way and construction. Eventually land script represented negotiable currency.

Seaberg's hotel was a continuing source of pride but at the same time a bottomless money pit hastened along by a decline in guest bookings and construction of another hotel by a business rival. As an attorney he had few peers. An area newspaper called him "broad-minded, liberal, conservative and generally correct in all advice to his clients." Just before the turn of the century Seaberg estimated his net worth at $40,000 (more than $1 million in today's dollars), a phenomenal achievement considering that just a few years before he had been a newly arrived immigrant with virtually nothing. It seemed that as long as the economy held strong all was possible. Dabbling in the stock market spotlighted the flawed policy he had begun to depend upon: depending entirely on borrowed capital to finance his enterprises.

"With only the strictest self-discipline could Hugo refrain from embarking on a venture that held some promise of success," says Preusser. That, as it turned out, was the Hotel Seaberg which he had been encouraged to build when the Santa Fe Railroad's Harvey House moved out from Raton. Expansion after expansion from 1903 until 1939 followed, always with borrowed money. During the course of his involvement with the hotel, Seaberg's enthusiasm and his boasting knew no limits. One advertisement for the hotel cafe read in part: "the most fastidious go away with a pleasant smile. It (the food) tickles their palates..." Eventually the hotel grew to 200 rooms, all with telephones. Seaberg's dream was to make his hotel "comparable to anything in Denver." As Preusser notes, "his optimism would not be bridled;" he refused to bask in past achievements.

One of these successes of course was in land script. Seaberg became one of its most successful and sought after buyers and sellers in the Southwest. Railroads were important to the settlement of the west. The undertaking carried its own reward both for the railroads and for the dealers in script. One of Seaberg's most noteworthy ventures in this field occurred when he purchased a major portion of the lieu rights for the Santa Fe Pacific Railroad, a subsidiary of the Santa Fe. The area involved was slightly less than ten million acres. Commissions varied from fifty to ten cents an acre, prices for the script itself varied from $2.50 to $9.50 per acre. Preusser notes that Seaberg's voluminous advertising, his knowledge of land law, and his connections with the Santa Fe Pacific, coupled with his unquenchable ambition, made his land script business the "most lucrative' of his career. His fertile imagination knew no boundaries. One of his more interesting ideas was to settle 10,000 Russian immigrant Jews on a 98,000 acre tract in Curry County. It, like so many of his other ideas, came to nothing. The script business was not always easy.

Sometimes selling script became vexing. In one venture Seaberg traveled to Detroit, then to San Francisco, then to Chicago, and finally back to Detroit to seal the deal, only to find that his seller had already sold to someone else. "I was completely taken off my feet," Seaberg confided to his friend Porter. However, he was not to be put off by such bumps in the road. Records show that in Colfax County alone, the county seat of Raton, 113,972 acres passed through his hands. He was a large landowner with property throughout New Mexico, Kansas, Texas, New Orleans, and Washington, D.C., much of it doubtless bought with other people's money. Such wheeling and dealing exacted both a physical and emotional stress, and he was hospitalized more than once with breakdowns. "This recent script game has been a nightmare," he confided before one such episode. Nonetheless, he added that " "If I could with a magic wand touch the heavens and see all my (land) patents shower down and thus clean up an agitation which has been very torturous I would still say that I have been very fortunate."

The period 1910-1920 in Raton allowed Seaberg to devote himself to his hotel and other business activities but also to become interested in Republican politics as well. That involvement sprung from the statehood movement. Unlike others, Seaberg opposed the idea because of a concern that taxes had become too high and that there were not enough taxpayers to pay them. He concluded that statehood, instead of serving as a stimulus for growth, would act as a depressant. Seaberg's interest in politics waxed and waned and chiefly involved the statehood issue. He was vehemently opposed to something called the "Blue Ballot," which addressed the ease with which the new constitution could be amended. He even ran a front page advertisement against it in his hometown newspaper, the *Raton Range*. The measure passed handily anyway. He also later carried on extensive correspondence with President Herbert Hoover's personal secretary to whom he passed on advice for the Chief Executive.

In his later years, Seaberg's abiding interest was in his beloved hotel, an enterprise, which while providing an outlet for his entrepreneurial genius and financing skills, proved his ultimate undoing. Seaberg always seemed to think the answer to his problems was adding on a few more rooms to increase occupancy and revenues, never seeming to realize that such undertakings cost money. Someone with his business acumen might have known better. When he was finished with the hotel—although it seemed he never was—Seaberg had spent untold thousands of dollars. When a rival group built a modern facility he was finished. "He had overextended himself and he knew it but, by late 1929, he could no longer do anything about it," writes Preusser. The financial burdens of the Depression era were too heavy. He was forced to sell up and liquidate everything.

After that, although he lingered several years until his death August 6, 1945, in Trinidad, Colorado, where he and his wife had moved, and no attempt to find work—any kind of work even manual labor at his advanced age—met with success. His pleadings dwindled to the downright pathetic. He sought work in the public sector, the private sector, and implored fellow New Mexico hotelier Conrad Hilton for a position. Two years before his death he wrote his daughter that "If you would tell me what factories are employing old men, I will make applications." He wrote the Civil Service Commission that he was willing to be sent "anywhere in the world," at a moment's notice, for a job. Nothing bore fruit. A sad end for a proud man.

Of him, Preusser wrote: "He had lived a full life, one which always excited and challenged him, and even though it treated him harshly and he wearied of it as he neared its end, it never <u>really</u> (author's underlining) defeated him. He had made his mark on a new land, from the country of his birth."

ARTHUR SELIGMAN, ESQ.,
SANTA FE

Arthur Seligman: Governor, banker, merchant

Arthur Seligman was the first non-Hispanic, native-born, Jewish governor of New Mexico (Office of the State Historian). A Democrat, he was elected to two terms by sweeping majorities but died in office. He was a populist-leaning progressive politician with a liberal bent who effected "many public improvements" as a leader in his home town of Santa Fe and in New Mexico. The *Las Vegas Optic* noted that Seligman had led the way toward better roads and bridges and construction of a new jail in Santa Fe without incurring "a cent of indebtedness" to the county.

In an inaugural address as governor in 1931 at the advent of the Depression he sought help from New Mexicans for the many problems confronting their state. He told them that "The governor...alone cannot produce the desired results. The legislature is not sufficient unto itself to accomplish them. The people...are the power behind the government. When an administration takes the people into its confidence...there need be no fear of failure." (State Historian)

Seligman, despite an upbringing of privilege and affluence as the scion of a wealthy merchant family and a Swarthmore College education, undertook sweeping programs to address New Mexico's economic woes. When he found that many of the state's rural children had little to eat and suffered from malnutrition or had little to wear except a flour sack, he responded with alacrity.

One response was to institute the state's first unemployment relief program in 1931. Another initiative was to establish vocational schools in rural Hispanic communities so students could learn traditional crafts which they could then market. But continuing shrinking tax revenues caused him to seek Federal aid which he saw as "a way to employ out-of-work New Mexicans, but also as a way to improve New Mexico's infrastructure." (State Historian)

Nonetheless, Seligman understood the need for fiscal responsibility. "No state," he stressed in his inaugural remarks, "should obligate itself to expend more money than can be reasonably expected from its citizens without hardship...New Mexico must live within her income." He understood that shrinking resources would lead to a shortfall in the state's tax base and that this, in turn, would impact New Mexico's ability to serve the state's most needy. (State Historian)

These programs were based on a solid foundation of achievement in city and county government in Santa Fe and as a successful businessman before he became Governor. He was president of Seligman Brothers from 1903–1926, president of the LaFonda Hotel, and president of the First National Bank of Santa Fe. Among his many elective offices were mayor of Santa Fe, chairman of the Santa Fe County Commission, president of the Education Service Commission, member of the New Mexico Board of Equalization, and chairman of the Democratic Central Committee.

Seligman's interests in the affairs of his city and state dated back to his formative years. In reporting on his death September 27, 1933, the Jewish Telegraphic Agency noted that "his (Seligman's) absorption in the public affairs of his state dates back to the time when he established a newspaper of his own, *The Evening Star of Santa Fe*, at the age of twelve."

He died on September 25, 1933, thirty minutes after delivering an address to the New Mexico Bankers Association in Albuquerque. He was sixty.

W. S. STRICKLER, ESQ.,
ALBUQUERQUE

Willard S(ackett). Strickler: Albuquerque businessman, banker

Like so many others who helped New Mexico grow, Willard S. Strickler followed a path of banking, business, and Republican politics to make it happen. Born in Junction City, Kansas, on July 14, 1863, he came to New Mexico Territory as a young man of twenty-one. Strickler entered business life as a bank clerk in his home town and continued that profession upon moving to Albuquerque as a teller at the Albuquerque National Bank.

He served with that institution until he organized the Bank of Commerce in 1890, with a post of cashier. Banking afforded him an opportunity to become involved in other business interests in Albuquerque, including owning a controlling interest in the *Albuquerque Evening Citizen* in 1905 of which he became president. His name ran on the masthead of the newspaper during his tenure as president. William S. Brogan was listed as managing editor.

In that same year he also organized the Electric Power Company in Albuquerque, which supplied electricity to the city. Strickler was an early advocate of recycling. *History of New Mexico* noted that he utilized the refuse from the American Lumber Company plant with other fuel. To what purpose the notation did not explain. Additionally, he was a founding member of the Albuquerque Commercial Club.

Strickler was a Republican and served several terms as Treasurer of the Bernalillo County Republican Party, city treasurer, and as a member of the Territorial Central Committee.

He died January 4, 1925, and is buried in Fairview Memorial Park Cemetery in Albuquerque.

HON. R. M. TURNER,
SILVER CITY

Robert M. Turner: Attorney, banker

In 1902, attorney Robert M. Turner gave the Commencement address to graduating students at the New Mexico Territorial Normal School in Silver City (now Western New Mexico University). His topic was "Opportunities." He must have felt that his opportunities lay elsewhere and in a different profession, however, because a few years later he was in another city and in banking instead of the law. Turner did remain in Silver City long enough after those graduation remarks to enter in a law partnership with James S. Fielder and get into politics.

On January 21, 1910 the *Silver City Enterprise* was reporting that Turner had moved to Hillsboro where he was vice president and cashier of the American National Bank there, but that he and an associate were planning to establish a new financial institution in El Paso to be known as the El Paso Bank and Trust Company. The bank was to be capitalized with $100,000 provided by group of New Mexico and Texas investors.

Two years later there was a reshuffling at the top. On May 1, 1912, the *Enterprise* told its readers that Turner had resigned his position and sold his interest to F.P. Jones of the Silver City wholesale grocery firm of Jones, Downes and Company. Turner, the newspaper noted, "who on account of ill health" was compelled to seek a lower altitude. That he did.

On August 22, 1933, the *Silver City Independent* reported Turner's death in Forest Grove, Oregon, at age sixty five. He had lived for a while in Arizona before returning to his native Pacific Northwest. The newspaper noted that Turner had been active in Republican politics in Silver City since his arrival in 1900, having been elected to the New Mexico House of Representatives in 1903 and twice Grant County Attorney. In Silver City, he had been active in the Masons, the Elks, and the Malta Commandery of the Knights Templar.

J. H. VAUGHN, ESQ.,
SANTA FE

John Howard Vaughn: Financier and capitalist

The *Santa Fe New Mexican*, on September 22, 1935, in reporting John Howard Vaughn's death summed up his life with this: "For half a century (he was) a well known citizen (of the city) who filled official positions with ability and integrity." He had just turned seventy-five. The *New Mexican* noted that Vaughn owed his fifty year career as a financier to early mentoring from United States Senator Stephen B. Elkins of West Virginia. As a youth, Vaughn attended a military institute near his home town of Port Chester, New York. This, the *New Mexican* observed, "was responsible for the straight and soldierly bearing which always characterized him." Likely Vaughn took this military discipline with him when he began his career in finance on Wall Street.

Upon leaving school he went to work for a tea broker. That led to meeting Elkins, with whom he worked two years before the senator dispatched him to Santa Fe for a position as assistant bookkeeper in the First National Bank. Elkins was chief stockholder and president of the bank, and he needed someone on the ground to look after his interests. Once at the bank, the newcomer soon gained positions of increasing responsibility and authority, successively becoming chief accountant, assistant cashier, and cashier. This led *Leading Facts of New Mexican History* to note his "marked business ability, initiative and enterprise." Vaughn's record of trust and integrity in the territory's principal bank, in turn, led to ever increasing positions in city and territorial financial affairs.

Fellow Republican Governor Miguel A. Otero appointed him treasurer of the territory, a post he filled from 1901 to 1909. He also served two years on the board of commissioners of the New Mexico penitentiary. After statehood, Vaughn headed the insurance department of the State Corporation Commission. The city of Santa Fe named him city treasurer. He was also a member of the board of education. In June of 1914 he was made acting postmaster in Santa Fe and served until November of that year.

The *New Mexican* concluded its obituary with "he was sort of an institution here (in Santa Fe) and his passing will bring a pang of regret..."

A good steward of private and public monies: Howard Vaughn.

HON. W. B. WALTON,
SILVER CITY

William B. Walton: Publisher, Congressman, public servant

Newspapering, the law, and Democratic politics were in William B. Walton's blood. He won more elections over his long political career than he lost. His 1918 U.S. Senate race was his first defeat for public office and it was to the formidable Republican powerhouse A.B. Fall. Fall, of course, later was to suffer disgrace in the Teapot Dome Scandal, but he was at the height of his political power when he bested Walton.

The loss was no more than a temporary setback for Walton. He had already served as New Mexico's representative in Congress during World War I, he owned the *Silver City Independent*, and he had already accomplished much, including service at the 1910 Constitution Convention, in the House and Senate in Santa Fe, and as district attorney.

Walton was born in Altoona, Pennsylvania, in 1871 and studied at the South Jersey Institute in Bridgeton, New Jersey. He moved to Deming in 1891 where the law and the newspaper business quickly gained his attention. As was common at that time, he studied the law under the direction of a practicing attorney. He was admitted to the New Mexico Bar in 1893. In the meantime, he also had dual responsibilities at the *Deming Headlight* as editorial director and head of the business office. He found journalism much to his liking and bought the paper in 1893. It marked the beginning of forty years of active newspaper ownership and involvement.

In 1895 he was appointed clerk of the Third Judicial District Court of New Mexico. Acceptance of that post meant a move to Silver City, where he was to continue following the law, politics, and journalism. He purchased the *Independent* in 1898.

His long and varied public service included an appointment by Governor Miguel A. Otero in 1903 as secretary to the Territorial Board of Managers for the Louisiana Purchase Exposition in St. Louis, presidency of the New Mexico Bar Association in 1913, and in 1918 service as president of the Board of Regents of the New Mexico Normal School, now Western New Mexico University.

Years later he was to comment in the pages of his newspaper on two facets of his life of which he was most proud: service in Congress where he helped prosecute a successful conclusion to World War I and work for the increase of pensions for veterans. Always mindful of veterans' contributions in 1920 he traveled to Washington to work with New Mexico's Congressional delegation to save Fort Bayard from neglect when its abandonment by the War Department was imminent. Through his efforts, the hospital was transferred to the Public Health Service and later to the Veterans Affairs Office. Fort Bayard remains in use today.

In March of 1932 and only seven years before his death he sought renomination as District Attorney in the Democratic primary. In a modest article in his own paper titled "A Record of Service," he extolled his forty years of public service. Soon, however, advancing age forced him to leave both public office and publishing.

When he finally exited the newspaper business in 1933 he chose to sell the *Independent* to Clyde E. Ely, an equally strong voice in New Mexico journalism. Ely soon converted the *Independent* from its weekly status to a daily, now the *Silver City Daily Press and Independent*.

Walton died April 14, 1939. The Elks Lodge and Masons of Silver City conducted his funeral services. He had held positions of leadership in both organizations.

GEORGE W. WARD, ESQ.,
LAS VEGAS

George W. Ward: Farmer, steward

George W. Ward was a successful dry land farmer in San Miguel County and a steward of the New Mexico Territorial Insane Asylum, now the State Hospital at Las Vegas.

He was a Republican and was active in city and county politics. He was a past grand master of the Masonic Lodge.

An imposing figure, the *Las Vegas Optic* had this to say of Ward in a front-page write-up of February 22, 1906: "a giant in body, a prince in disposition, gentleman by nature and birth and breeding."

Suggested Further Reading

Compiled by Bruce Wilson

Note: Websites current at time of publication.

"abcreads: Albuquerque Libraries: It's a Grand Old History." accessed May 5, 2013. http://abcreads.blogspot.com/2011/07/albuquerque-libraries-its-grand-old.html.

Anderson, George B. *History of New Mexico: Its Resources and People, Volume I*. Los Angeles: Pacific States Press, 1907.

_____. *History of New Mexico: Its Resources and People, Volume II*. Los Angeles: Pacific States Press, 1907.

"Annual New Mexico Fair Opens Today." *Albuquerque Morning Journal*, September 18, 1905.

Archive Grid. "Secundino Romero Papers, 1824–1911, (bulk 1885–1911)." accessed March 18, 2013. http:beta.worldcat.org/archivegrid/collection/data/43414321.

_____. "William H. Andrews papers, 1871–1912." accessed May 6, 2013. http://beta.worldcat.org/archivegrid/data/40966640.

"Asks That Body of Husband Be Buried Beside Her Grave." *Albuquerque Morning News*, January 21, 1921.

Ball, Larry D. *Desert Lawmen: The High Sheriffs of New Mexico and Arizona 1846–1912*. Albuquerque: University of New Mexico Press, 1992.

_____. *The United States Marshals of New Mexico & Arizona Territories 1846–1912*. Albuquerque: University of New Mexico Press, 1978.

Bartleby.com. "Roosevelt, Theodore, 1899. The Rough Riders: Appendix A. Muster-Out Roll: Troop H." accessed March 9, 2013. www.bartleby.com/51/ah.html.

Bullis, Don. *New Mexico Historical Biographies*. Albuquerque: Rio Grande Books, 2011.

"Changes Ordered in National Guard." *Albuquerque Citizen*, October 31, 1907, page 6.

Crafton, Donald. *Before Mickey: the Animated Film 1898–1928*. The University of Chicago Press, 1993.

City of Albuquerque, New Mexico Certificate and Record of Death, September 27, 1909, certificate number 2784.

City of Albuquerque, New Mexico Certificate and Record of Death, August 13, 1917, certificate number 8264.

CNN iReport. "Earl Stevenson commissioned as Colonel by New Mexico Governor." accessed May 2, 2013. http://ireport.cnn.com/docs/DOC-888656.

"Col. W. H. Greer Passes Away in New York." *Albuquerque Morning Journal*, September 24, 1910.

"Col. Porterfield, Silver City Pioneer, Called by Death." *Silver City Enterprise*, January 14, 1943.

"Col. George W. Prichard Dies; State Loses Another Old-Timer in Famous Lawyer and Orator." *Santa Fe New Mexican*, February 15, 1935.

"Dammer Sells His Interests to Buddecke." *Albuquerque Evening Citizen*, April 6, 1906.

Dargan, Marion. "The Attitude of the Territorial Press, 1895–1901. accessed May 4, 2013. www.newmexicohistory.org/centennial/Statehood/Statehood-2.html.

Dean, Rob, Editor. *Santa Fe Its 400th Year: Exploring the Past, Defining the Future*. Santa Fe: Sunstone Press, 2010.

"Death Calls Col. Howard H. Betts." *Silver City Enterprise*, October 5, 1923.

"Death of A.B. Baca." *The Socorro Chieftain*, July 29, 1916.

"Educational Pioneer Dies; Veteran Hiram Hadley Passes." *Santa Fe New Mexican*, December 4, 1922.

Eveleth, Robert W. "A Biography of Cony Thomas Brown: the New Mexico School of Mines Best Friend and Benefactor." New Mexico Bureau of Geology & Mineral Resources, Socorro, New Mexico, May 2010.

FamilySearch. "Robert W. Hopkins, 'United States Census, 1910.'" accessed March 19, 2013. https://familysearch.org/pal:/MM9.1.1/MGSC-YNK.

FindaGrave. "Edward G. Murphey." accessed May 24, 2013. www.findagrave.com/cgi bin/fg.cgi?page=gr&GSln=MU&GSpartial=1&GSbyrel=al...

_____. "Judge Frank W. Parker." www.findagrave.com/

Fleming, Elvis E. and Ernestine Chesser Williams. *Treasures of History II: Chaves County Vignettes*. Roswell: Chaves County Historical Society, 1991.

_____. *Treasures of History IV: Historical Events of Chaves County, New Mexico*. Lincoln, NE: iUniverse, Inc., 2003.

"Funeral of Pioneer Las Vegas Man Held." *Albuquerque Morning Journal*, June 5, 1920.

GenealogyVillage. "Three Las Vegas Cemeteries: San Miguel County: NMG, Vol. XXX, No.3, Sep 1991, page 64." accessed March 27, 2013. http://nmahgpgenealogy.village.com/sanmiguel/three_lasvegascems3.htm.

_____. "History Bernalillo." accessed March 19, 2013. http://nmahgp.genealogy.village.com/bernalillo/postoffice_bernalillo.htm.

Gifford, Denis. *American Animated Films: The Silent Era, 1897-1929*. Jefferson, North Carolina: McFarland & Company, Inc., Publishers, 1900.

Glasrud, Bruce A. *African American History in New Mexico: Portraits from Five Hundred Years*. Albuquerque: University of New Mexico Press, 2013.

"Gov. Arthur Seligman Dead; Was Outstanding Figure in New Mexico's Growth." *Jewish Telegraphic Agency*. September 27, 1933.

Hamm, Ron. *The Bursums of New Mexico: Four Generations of Leadership and Service*. Socorro, New Mexico: Manzanares Publishing, 2012.

_____. "A.B. Baca's Uncle Elfego." *New Mexico Magazine* 59 12, December 1981, 24.

Haywood Trial Gallery. "Big Bill Haywood Trial." Idanha Witness to History. accessed May 30, 2013.

Historic American Buildings Survey. "First National Bank Building (Star Jewelry) 100-102 East San Antonio Avenue, El Paso, El Paso County, Texas." HABS No. TX-3308.

History of Animation. A2ZCDS, 2005.

"Hopewell Buried with Masonic Honors." *Albuquerque Morning Journal*, August 15, 1919.

Hornung, Chuck. *Fullerton's Rangers: A History of the New Mexico Territorial Mounted Police*. Jefferson, North Carolina: McFarland & Company, Inc., Publishers, 2005. 49.

Idaho Public Television. "Harry Orchard: The assassin and chief prosecution witness." Accessed May 31, 2013. http://idahoptv.org/productions/specials/trial/thetrial/orchard.cfm.

"Judge William H. Newcomb is Dead." *Silver City Independent*, June 19, 1917.

Julian, George W. "Land-Stealing in New Mexico." *The North American Review*, Volume 0145 Issue 368 (July 1887), 17-32.

Keleher, William A. *Memoirs: 1892-1969, A New Mexico Item*. Albuquerque: University of New Mexico Press, 1969. New Edition, Santa Fe: Sunstone Press, 2008.

Kropp, Simon F. "Hiram Hadley and the Founding of New Mexico State University." *Arizona and the West* 9 1 (Spring, 1967), 21-40.

Lamar, Howard Roberts. *The Far Southwest 1846-1912: A Territorial History*. Albuquerque: University of New Mexico Press, 2000.

"Las Vegas Light and Fuel Company Sold." *Albuquerque Evening Citizen*, December 25, 1905.

Legislative Assembly of the Territory of New Mexico. "An Act for the relief of A.B. Baca for services in pursuing, arresting and returning to the jail of Santa Fe County, Jose Telles, an escaped prisoner accused of murder. H.B. No. 91: Approved February 28, 1903."

Levy, Felice D. *Obituaries On File*. New York: Facts on File, 1979.

Lopez, Jesus L. "Don Miguel arrives, a dynasty is born." *Las Vegas Optic*, October, 2011

"Lubin Company." *Silver City Independent*. December 21, 1915.

McNary, James Graham. *This is My Life*. Albuquerque: University of New Mexico Press, 1956.

Melzer, Richard and Robert J. Tórrez. *A History of New Mexico Since Statehood*. Albuquerque: University of New Mexico Press, 2011.

Metz, Leon Claire. *The Shooters*. El Paso: Mangan Books, 1976.

"Mora Electric Will Be Built." *Albuquerque Citizen*, November 2, 1907.

"Nature Exacts Final Tribute From Colonel Max. Frost." *Santa Fe New Mexican*, October 14, 1909.

New Mexico Office of the State Historian. "Fairview Cemetery." accessed May 19, 2011. www.newmexicohistory.org/filedetails_docs.php?fileID=9948.

_____. "Hagerman, Herbert James: 1906:1907." accessed May 24, 2013. www.newmexicohistory.org/filedetails.php?fileID=23590.

_____. "Hillsboro Murder, 1907." accessed May 7, 2013. www.newmexicohistory.org/filedetails.php?fileID=21648.

_____. "King Solomon's Mysterious Demise." accessed May 21, 2013. www.newmexicohistory.org/filedetails.php?fileID=23423.

_____. "New Mexico's Fight for Statehood 1895–1912, Part I." accessed April 2, 2011. newmexicohistory.org/file.

_____. "Seligman, Arthur." accessed May 24, 2013. www.newmexicohistory.org/filedetails.php?fileID=23514.

_____. "Solomon Luna, Chapter I: Solomon's Ancestry." accessed May 21, 2013. http://newmexicohistory.org/filedetails.ph;?fileID=21653.

_____. "Solomon Luna, Chapter V: Political Career. accessed February 17, 2013. http://newmexicohistory.org/filedetails.ph;?fileID=21662.

_____. "Twitchell, Ralph Emerson." accessed March 28, 2013. www.newmexicohistory.org/filedetails.php?fileID=21280.

New Mexico State University. "A History of the Department of Mathematical Sciences 1888 1965: Appendix C: Tributes to Hiram Hadley." accessed February 27, 2013. www.nmsu.edu/alumni/Hadley.html.

New Mexico's Statehood: 100 years of Enchantment. "Eugenio Romero." accessed May 5, 2013. www.newmexicohistoryorg/centennial/Delegates/Bio-Romero-Eugenio.html.

Origins of American Animation: Notes. "Notes on the origins of American Animation, 1900–1921." accessed March 31, 2012. http://memory.loc.gov/ammem/oahtml/oapres.html.

Otero, Miguel A. *My Life on the Frontier, 1882–1897*. Santa Fe: Sunstone Press, 2007.

Owen, Gordon. *Las Cruces, New Mexico 1849–1999: Multi-Cultural Crossroads*. Las Cruces: Red Sky Publishing Co., 1999.

Palmer, Harry S. *New Mexico Men of Affairs in Caricature: the Optic Cartoon Book*. Las Vegas, New Mexico: Las Vegas Optic, 1906.

Peterson, C.S. *Representative New Mexicans*. Charleston, South Carolina: Nabu Press, 1912.

"Pioneer of East Las Vegas Dies Suddenly." *Albuquerque Morning Journal*, June 2, 1920.

PoliticalGraveyard.com. "Politicians in Railroading in New Mexico." accessed May 12, 2013. http://politicalgraveyard.com/geo/NM/railroading.html.

Pope, Judge John W. "New Mexico's Man for All Seasons: Judge Luis Armijo of Las Vegas." *Bar Journal*. May/June 1996, 17-18.

Preusser, Meldon J. "Hugo Seaberg, New Mexico Capitalist, 1869–1945. A Thesis Presented to the Faculty of the Graduate School of Arts and Sciences, University of Denver." December, 1968.

Reynolds, Betty Blakslee. *Anna K. Brown: A Pioneer Socorro Volunteer*. Socorro, New Mexico: New Mexico Tech Library, 1997.

"Robert Hopkins Dies; Funeral On Wednesday." *El Paso Herald*, November 16, 1920.

Rootsweb. "Edward A. Cahoon." accessed March 9, 2013. www.bartleby.com/51.ah.html.

Sager, Stan. ¡*Viva Elfego!: The Case for Elfego Baca, Hispanic Hero*. Santa Fe: Sunstone Press, 2012.

"Sen. Elkins Launched Howard Vaughn on Bank Career Here" *Santa Fe New Mexican*, September 22, 1936.

Spanish American War Centennial Website. "Colonel William H. H. Llewellyn: Troop H, 1st U.S. Cavalry ("Rough Riders")." accessed February 17, 2013. www.spanamwar.com/rrmllewellyn.htm.

"State News." *Deming Headlight*, May 24, 1913.

The Animated Cartoon Factory—History of Animation Timeline. "History of Animation 1911–1920." accessed March 31, 2012. www.brianlemay.com/History/timeline 1911–1920.html.

"The Armstrong Report Comes Out." *The New York Times*, February 23, 1906.

"The Birth of a Partisan Judiciary, 1910–1911." *New Mexico Law Review*. (October, 1975, 1-14.)

"The Electric Light Plant." *The Socorro Chieftain*, February 22, 1908.

"The Grand Lodge." *Albuquerque Daily Citizen*, October 15, 1896.

"The Hard Way." *The Albuquerque Citizen*, December 18, 1907.

The Past 100 Years. "The Past 100 Years." accessed May 19, 2011. www.thefreelibrary.com/THE+PAST+100+YEARS-a0212072403.

"Turquoise Gems Attract Notice In Displays and Mine at the Exposition." *Silver City Independent*, August 23, 1904.

Twitchell, Ralph Emerson. *The Leading Facts of New Mexican History, Volume II*. New Edition, Santa Fe: Sunstone Press, 2007.

_____. *The Leading Facts of New Mexican History, Volume III*. Cedar Rapids: The Torch Press 1917. New Edition, Santa Fe: Sunstone Press, 2014.

_____. *The Leading Facts of New Mexican History, Volume IV*. Cedar Rapids: The Torch Press, 1917. New Edition, Santa Fe: Sunstone Press, 2014.

_____. *The Leading Facts of New Mexican History, Volume V.* Cedar Rapids: The Torch Press, 1917. New Edition, Santa Fe: Sunstone Press, 2014.

_____. "Automobiles and the Willows." accessed May 11, 2013. www.vocesdesantafe.org/social/index.php/explore-our-history/family-histories.

Wikipedia. "Arthur Seligman." accessed February 17, 2013. http://en.wikipedia.org/wiki/Arthur_Seligman.

_____. "Elfego Baca." accessed August 22, 2012. http://en.wikipedia.org/wiki/Elfego_Baca.

_____. "Miguel Antonio Otero (born 1859)." accessed February 17, 2013. http://en.wikipedia.org/wiki/Miguel_Antonio_Otero_(II).

_____. "National Irrigation Congress." accessed March 2, 2013. http://en.wikipedia.org/wiki/National_Irrigation_congress.

_____. "New Mexico State University." accessed April 23, 2013. http://en.wikipedia.org/wiki/New_Mexico_State_University.

_____. "Ralph E. Twitchell." accessed February 17, 2013. http://en.wikipedia.org/wiki/Ralph_E._Twitchell.

_____. "William J. Mills." accessed August 22, 2012. https://en.wikipedia.org/wiki/William_J._Mills.

www.ingramcontent.com/pod-product-compliance
Lightning Source LLC
Chambersburg PA
CBHW080441170426
43195CB00017B/2851